1P 92 25 —

22 ^{50}

=X

THE SUFFERING GOD

THE SUFFERING GOD

*Selected Letters to Galatea
and to Papastephanou*

Nikos Kazantzakis

*Translated by
Philip Ramp
and
Katerina Anghelaki Rooke*

*Introduction by
Katerina Anghelaki Rooke*

CARATZAS BROTHERS, PUBLISHERS
NEW ROCHELLE, NEW YORK
1979

ENGLISH TRANSLATION COPYRIGHT © 1979
        BY KATERINA ANGHELAKI ROOKE AND PHILIP RAMP
ORIGINAL GREEK LANGUAGE EDITION © 1958
        BY HELEN KAZANTZAKIS

LIBRARY OF CONGRESS
CATALOG CARD NUMBER: 78-75133

ISBN: 0-89241-088-4

CARATZAS BROTHERS, PUBLISHERS
481 MAIN STREET
NEW ROCHELLE, NEW YORK 10801

Editor's Note

The letters to Emmanuel Papastephanou were first published by Kyriakos Mitsotakis in the Greek magazine *Epikaira*. The letters in this book follow the same sequence in which they were published there.

The letters to Galatea were first published in Greek in 1958 under the title *Epistoles pros te Galateia* (Letters to Galatea) by the publishing house "Difros". The edition and notes were prepared by Ares Diktaios; this book follows the same numbering sequence for the letters.

The editors of this book have deleted letters, and parts of letters, which they believed detracted from its thematic unity. The symbol used to show ellipses of parts of letters is three asterisks (* * *).

A note on style: The letters follow fairly random structures; in some instances they are dated, with a salutation and fairly formal closing remarks. At other times the dates are missing, while additional remarks are appended after the signature. Finally, in some instances, there is no signature at all.

CONTENTS

Introduction

I.

Each time we concern ourselves with the work of an artist and try to identify the message and the contribution of his art we are, at the same time, seeking the real face of the poet. And each time, with varied intensity, arises the question: where is the essence of his personality to be found? In his life or in his work? In his work where everything has been crystallized into a new reality or in his life where we have the basic elements of his creativity before they are altered by the process of art?

The answer to such a question is neither easy nor conclusive and we often turn to the private correspondence of the artist for enlightenment and guidance. For letters are by their nature in a half-way state; they are neither a complete work of art open to judgment and criticism nor an absolutely secret and unrevealed side of the creator. Letters stand somewhere between what is conscious and what is unconscious, what is personal and what has become public because of the further development of the artist.

1920-1924 were decisive years both in Greek and Western history. They were also crucial years in the life and work of Kazantzakis when the Idea ripened which was to hold together all his work till the end of his life. From that very important period, during which Kazantzakis, nearly 40 years old, was in the middle of an agitated and constantly changing Europe, we really have no other record except the letters to his first wife Galatea,[1] a few letters to a distant, childhood friend in America, the priest Manolis Papastephanou and a small book[2] in the form of a dialogue, where five people talk about God.

Most of the letters to Galatea were written from May,

1921 to November, 1923. Kazantzakis writes to his wife in Athens first from Austria and then from Germany. The more one studies these letters, the more strongly one feels the need of Galatea's replies which, unfortunately, no longer exist. Thus the personality of the woman who was Kazantzakis' "Comrade" for 14 years remains vague and becomes confused through the contradictory opinions of friends and enemies. As for her way of seeing Kazantzakis, here again we are at a loss because of the complete demystification she later performed on her husband. Whatever they had in common in their destiny and their origin lost its weight, little by little, as their personalities developed in totally different directions and their relationship became antagonistic. From these pages of cosmogony and theogony often emanates the bitterness of a man whose questions are never answered and whose agony is never comprehended. During the 14 years of their marriage they seldom shared a common life. Kazantzakis travelled most of the time pushed on not only by a relentless need to search, but also by a feeling that their life together was a failure. There was very little left which could recall the two young people in Heraklion at the dawn of this century who, when still in High School, entered hand in hand the magic world of poetry and published, nearly simultaneously, their first creations.[3]

A very important role in their relationship was played by Kazantzakis' father, who fell like a heavy shadow on Kazantzakis' life. An old warrior, formidable and severe, he was a real terror to the women in the house[4] and had a particular weakness for his only son. This father was to come to life again much later in one of Kazantzakis' novels as Kapetan Michaelis. After living together for a year in Athens, Galatea and Nikos got married in Crete in June, 1911, in a small ceremony without much publicity, mainly because they married against the wishes of Kazantzakis' father.

To what extent is it possible for one to go deep into the private life of a creator and reconstruct a reality which will never go beyond the realm of guesses? And furthermore, what is the real value of all these speculations in relation to the understanding of a work of art? We know, first of all, that their temperaments were diametrically opposed. She was a woman of quick mind, realistic, with both feet on the ground, energetic, lively and with her own artistic ambitions. He was a visionary, passionately metaphysical, constantly kneading and moulding the face of his God. She was probably well aware that in art she would stop half-way, somewhere between the great Yes and the horrid No. She knew that Kazantzakis would finally leave behind a major work which would justify him. By "major work" we mean here not so much the real value of a work of art, which is always open to discussion and re-evaluation, but a work which is characterized by an intensity of inspiration and an overwhelming personal vision. No one can deny Kazantzakis these qualities. This difference of dimension alone was a sufficient reason to embitter a relationship which was rapidly going to descend from the beautiful clouds of adolescence to daily friction, antagonism and anguish.

So Kazantzakis travelled — to Mount Athos, the Peloponnesus, Switzerland, the Caucasus and then to Austria and Germany, hence most of these letters.[5] We know the importance of new landscapes for Kazantzakis: "Travelling and Confession (creation being the highest and most exact form of confession) have been the two greatest joys of my life. To wander over the earth; to see and never have my fill of seeing. . ."[6]

Nevertheless, his stay in Austria and Germany was something more than "seeing". It was the time and place where deep wells of knowledge opened in front of him. Western Europe was then a blazing cauldron and in the middle of it the poet was leading a double struggle. First, there was his inner anguish to give his work a solid backbone and to clarify his Idea, and secondly his desire to reconcile two equally strong voices in him: art and religion, or what he called the Cry, "I will never find the coherent Word to liberate the Cry that tears my entrails apart. But I will constantly besiege its meaning, as well as I can, through works of art and maybe someone better than me will be victorious."[7] Defeated in the First World War, bankrupt, immersed in hunger and misery, Germany and Austria were in a state of collapse. "The horror of the collapse of Vienna is beyond description. A special service was organized by the police to stop people from throwing themselves into the Danube at night."[8]

Deprived of all comfort, often in a cold room, even sick sometimes (there was the unbearable skin disease in Vienna which we will discuss in more detail, further on) Kazantzakis fought on with the only weapons he had, his "24 soldiers" as he called the 24 letters of the Greek alphabet. He fought with them, he was faithful to them and at the same time he was ashamed of them. In this notion of "shame", when his calling seemed a retreat, one can find the key to the further development of his philosophy and for his attitude toward his wife as it appears in these letters.

Galatea, besides being his wife, had become a kind of symbol, as often happens when a very close person loses his specific weight, his character or features and becomes an idea. It represents, that is, an outlook toward life which, when combined at a certain psychological moment with our own, offers us a new vision, a new approach to life. The object of love and concentration is not any longer a particular person but the elements which characterize him. The role he plays in one's life is somehow equivalent to the role that those elements play in the whole movement of the world.

What Kazantzakis saw in Galatea at those times was an energy, an active power, a force which was able to turn ideas into reality, ideology into action. It is true that in those

days Galatea was one of the very few women in Greece who
had the courage to be very outspoken about her political
ideas, to be at the head of the various progressive
organizations and to support, with her presence, any
revolutionary movement. Later on she was persecuted for
her communist ideas but never got to the point of being
imprisoned or exiled. So Kazantzakis, in his best moments,
turned towards her hoping for help in situations where he
felt hesitant and closed in himself. In his worst moments he
saw in her a challenge and a complete lack of understanding
which filled him with bitterness.

Kazantzakis was going through one of the most
important changes in his life. Deeply shaken by what he felt
was a new Middle Ages in Europe, he was slowly coming out
of the Buddhic cloud wherein he had dwelt for some time
thinking he could find there an answer to the problem of
existence. The world then ceased to be a phantasmagoria, a
dream to be dissipated by the slightest breeze. Surrounded
by human suffering, Kazantzakis became more aware than
ever of the historical reponsibility of the individual which
makes each one feel that he has the answer to the injustice
of the world. It is a terrible moment when the artist begins
to suspect that in the scale of values man stands higher than
art so that in the end art cannot be used as an excuse for
not participating in history. The more pure and real the
clash between the eternal element (which is the natural
psychological climate of the artist) and the mortal element is,
the more pure and real is the personality of the creator. The
clash is unavoidable and its outcome may not be ultimately
so important. But in the narrow span of a life it expresses
more than the ideas of the artist. It expresses the form of his
soul.

The inner struggle of Kazantzakis during this period is
evident in all his writings. It fills him with anguish and drives
him from extreme hope to extreme despair. Because when
one focuses one's creativity and interest on the amelioration

of human fate, when the creation of hope becomes the target of one's endeavor, then one is automatically faced with another problem: Which cause to serve? Which one among all the forms of salvation that man has invented is the one which guarantees most effectiveness and can inspire most faith?

The Europe of 1922 was just coming out of the slow death of the First World War and was turning its eyes toward Russia. There, for the first time, history had taken the shape of faith. Human concern was not to be limited geographically. It was world-wide. And even as Kazantzakis, like the butterfly (a metaphor he loved so much), was coming out of the cocoon of Buddha, he was tentatively testing his wings for Russia and the new renaissance. The contrast between this hope and the awareness of the death of our civilization is one of the most striking and prophetic elements of these letters. Again and again he repeats that our western civilization is dying and with it, museums, works of art, the arabesques of imagination and logic; beauty had been transformed into aestheticism, morality into morals, generosity into charity. Where had Plato, Aristotle, Raphael and Vivaldi led? To form, to shapes, to empty snakeskins, to a society based on the evergrowing gap between victim and torturer, oppressor and oppressed, master and slave. It all added up to this feeling of the powerlessness of the individual to change the basic structure of a society which consisted of personal interest, greed and exploitation.

It was as if the whole structure was collapsing, revealing to Kazantzakis a decomposing world. A group of young Jewish girls inflamed by the idea of revolution played an important part in this revelation. Rachel, Itka, Dina and Rosa surrounded him with their tenderness and admiration but also with their fighting spirit. They led him to the slums, they introduced him to poverty and hunger, to demonstrations and to conferences where young people were no longer trying to correct things but were aiming at the complete destruction of the cannibalistic mechanism of their society. The Buddhic smile was no solution, for it seemed to be made of the stuff of cowardice. For Kazantzakis, Lenin took Buddha's place and behind Lenin stood the whole of Russia. Kazantzakis was later to say that in past times humanity was hoping for a redeemer to give it new life and save it; Moses, Christ, Muhammed. Now a whole nation had undertaken this frightening role with one soul and one body: Russia.

Thus Kazantzakis went about rejecting the cultural matter which had created him and in which he had begun his creative life. He even rejected art (his kernel of existence up to then) as being a product of a particular culture and society. All three formed a whole which for Kazantzakis had death as its only future. He felt united with all the "humiliated and the wronged" of this earth, the Jews, the workers, the poor, united with them in their yearning to receive the light from Russia which was invested with a new mysticism. He felt one with all the newborn powers, which still unshaped and unformed, were struggling for form, struggling to predominate and secure their power so that new elements could arise to fight the rules of yesterday and start again the same cycle. This historical vision, intensely echoing Spengler's theory of "historical comparative morphology" (widely read at that time) whereby civilizations, just like mortal organisms, complete the same cycle of birth, growth, decay and death, was to take, in The Saviors of God, further metaphysical extension and be (somehow) identified as the manifestation of the struggling God on this earth.

The spiritual realm of The Saviors is composed of this disputed weight whose center of gravity is one moment the individual and the next humanity. For a while the cry, "I want to be useful", covers the cry, "I want to become spirit". The liberation, realization and ascent of man must be used not only for a personal beatitude but must be put at the service of an idea. We are at the point where a "personal vision" clearly distinguishes itself from "an ideal" since the latter refers to humanity and to the means for its salvation that an individual can visualize. For Kazantzakis this Idea had, by now, the clearly defined features of communism but the way to realize it, that is, action, remained to be effected. A wholesome, total action was needed wherein the individual, even if it became merely an instrument, would not revolt because it would recognize an imperative above itself.

This was the point where Kazantzakis had the most difficulties. His very nature, his visionary essence, were the obstacle. His whole psychic mechanism was deeply interior and really shined only on his own climate of recollection. Thus action became for Kazantzakis the great ideal. Here we should probably mention Galatea again in as far as these letters of Kazantzakis express the deepest admiration for her. He was convinced that she was the one who would turn the ideology they had in common into reality, that she was the one who would serve it by her action. At the same time she was a person who had a value in herself, a value worth preserving, worth helping to bloom, worth saving from the corruption of the completely destructive atmosphere of intellectual Athens of those times.

One could venture to say that there is a parallel to be drawn between Kazantzakis' feelings for Galatea and those he had for Greece. He kept them both at the same distance and felt for both nostalgia alternating with bitterness, anger and sometimes contempt. Kazantzakis lived away from Greece for many years and during the last ten years of his life he never saw his native land. "I keep Greece under my eyelids" he used to say, "I don't have to go and see it." He often talked about Arab blood running in his veins and he also spoke a good deal about his native island, Crete. "I am Cretan" he often said, "not Greek", and actually felt that he was born at the crossroads of East and West and thus was by definition attempting the impossible synthesis between passion and intellect, life and death. It is what he called "The

Cretan glance" which was revealed to him while looking at a Minoan fresco, "The Jump of Death", showing a youth jumping over a sacrificial bull in a game of death transformed into art.

These are the recurrent points of reference for Kazantzakis, at least in what concerns his origin. As for Greece, it never created a favorable climate for him; starting with Galatea (who basically would not acknowledge him either as a person — she felt he was closed in himself, inhuman and without real concern for his fellow men — or as a writer — she felt he was pompous, rhetorical, unrealistic and, all in all, a dry intellectual) and ending with the intellectual clique of the country which, on the whole, remained indifferent to Kazantzakis' work. Indeed, it is rather odd to think that this man who passionately devoted himself to the Greek language, who, maybe more that any other Greek writer, strove to increase its richness and its linguistic capital, that he was accused of lack of Greek feeling, lack of language-sensitivity, even barbarism. All this, together with his refusal to enlist himself in any political party or to allow his ideology to become an instrument in the hands of this or that political leader, can in part explain Kazantzakis' somehow distant attitude towards Greece.

At the time when these letters were written Greece was going through one of the bitterest tragedies of its history: The catastrophe in Asia Minor changed, seemingly unalterably, the course of modern Greek history. It resulted in the uprooting of Ionian Hellenism and in internal political, and spiritual, collapse.

The story goes as far back as 1915, when King Constantine of Greece, who was married to the sister of the Kaiser, was a strong advocate of Greek neutrality (which was widely perceived as a pro-German position). On the other hand, Venizelos, the greatest political figure in the history of Modern Greece, was openly on the side of the Allies, especially the British. This situation started a long process of diplomatic maneuvering. Venizelos asked for the land along the Sea of Marmara and Ionia, the cradle of Greek civilization, in return for Greek participation in the war. In September, 1916, the discord between the King and Venizelos resulted in a final rupture; Venizelos seized Salonika by force and made it his capital, and Greece eventually joined the war on the side of the Allies in June, 1917.

Greece's participation was an important factor in the victory of the Allies on the Macedonian front. Then the moment of reward came. On May 2, 1919, the liberation of Smyrna took place. The Allies decided to disregard their objections to the King just to keep Venizelos in power. These were objections based on a new reality: The political scene had changed since 1915 when the idea had been born. The star of Kemal Ataturk was rising, advancing and gaining ground in the interior of Anatolia. Lenin's Russia was supporting and backing him. Even some of the Allies, particularly France, had good relations with Kemal. This was one more reason making the realization of the state of Armenia impossible though it had been created on paper by the treaty of Sevres.

The precarious situation of the Greeks in Asia Minor led to the first victories being followed by the retreat at the Sancarius river and Kemal's approach to Smyrna. The foreign powers and the representatives of mainland Greece observed the approaching catastrophe with seeming unconcern. It took hardly a month (from August 13, 1922, the day of Kemal's first attack on Afion Karahisar, to September 13) to reach Smyrna, the pearl of Anatolia, and turn it into a heap of ashes. Who was to blame for this holocaust, for the thousands of bodies floating in the sea with their throats cut, for the boats which never arrived, or arrived too late, from mother Greece to save the Greeks from the fury of the Turks? Who was to blame for the complete uprooting of Hellenism from the Soul of Ionia? Six generals and politicians were tried, judged responsible for the destruction and executed as traitors to Greece.

The real responsibility, though, lay much deeper. Political cliques, political hatred, personal ambitions and interest were the real motives for the actions of all, Greeks and foreign powers, in this tragic development of a nationalistic ideal probably doomed to failure from the first moment of its conception. This, more or less, was Kazantzakis' reaction to events. Disgusted, sad and horrified, he felt at the same time incapable of becoming fanatically involved in any group of people or ideas and fight. "But I myself alone cannot make contact with men, nor fight against indifference, ridicule and everyday small talk."[9] It is not that he did not care about the suffering of his race but even stronger than his sadness was his agony to see clearly, to place himself at a spot outside of time or place where all this mutual slaughtering of mankind would make some sense, where a driving force would be discernible. "It's Man I think about, Man — whether he be Turk, Greek, Jew or whatever. We must save him."[10]

Kazantzakis felt he was situated at an earthquake center. "I don't know how this earthquake appears in Greece, but here the chaos is visible and tangible and the agonies for a new order most deep."[11] A different wind blew in him, around him. From this perspective, he saw his compatriots as petty and narrow-minded, wasting their strength in political disputes at a crucial moment in their history, and at the same time he yearned to give them a new faith and save them. Faith and salvation could not be conceived of by Kazantzakis within the narrow limits of a nation. His vision included all men in a common effort, a common struggle. "It is Man we suffer for, Man we fight for, not for wretched, petty men."[12]

Greece alone cannot be saved, he said, all nations must be saved together or perish. Here Kazantzakis is talking in his own way about the mystery of the Greek race which has its own peculiar biochemistry. Mystery is probably not such a strong word when one recalls the deep schizophrenia of a nation which feels young and old at the same time, both from the historical and the psychological point of view. "The ancient statues and the contemporary sorrow", as another Greek poet, Seferis, put it, "represent a feeling of an archaetypal stretch in time," meaning that one can lean back in history and feel at ease with the origins of things there — while on the other hand the narrowness and predictability of the contemporary period weighs heavily upon the Greek consciousness.

It is not so much that ancient Greece represents a golden era in the mind of the Greek, a kind of lost paradise. It is mostly a memory of power versus a sense of powerlessness. Because what matters even more than the cultural radiation of a nation that shone so brightly at a certain moment in the history of mankind is the idea that at that time Greeks were masters of their own destiny, they were making their own future and shaping the features of their profile. In 1821, after 400 years of Turkish occupation, the Greeks regained their independence and the new state of Greece was founded.

It is impossible to examine here the complex question of the development of Greek consciousness during those 400 years, and, for that matter, the preceding Byzantine period. What could be said, at the risk of sounding arbitrary, is that during those long years the Greek lost his confidence in any collective reality which would represent his identity and felt that only as an individual could he safeguard his personal and his ethnic survival. Hence the extreme individualism of the Greek character. He can turn to his compatriots only in moments of crisis, while togetherness only means struggle and danger. In moments of peace he goes back to himself and looking after his own interests and thoroughly distrusting any activity or organization which would not be under his direct control. Thus on the one hand we have an admirable survival of the Greek substance, language and tradition and on the other a lack of confidence in what the Greeks themselves maintained and kept. Pride and frustration, two elements coexisting in the Greek consciousness, could partly at least explain what Kazantzakis called in these letters "the wretchedness of the Greek." And at that point he was right to think that Greeece alone cannot be saved. He had already entered the realm of *The Saviors of God.*.

II.

These letters would probably not be as important as they are if they were not also, in a way, the Odyssey of *The Saviors of God*. The seed of *The Saviors* began ripening in Kazantzakis in Vienna during his afflication with a peculiar skin disease that he described much later in his novel *Christ Recrucified*. Was it eczema or not? His face became swollen, and then like an open wound full of pus. Medicine and salves proved to be of no use. The psychiatrist Stekel diagnosed his psychic movement as "beyond the normal" and said his body was paying the price. It was like a miracle when he was cured after he left Vienna in August, 1922. In *Report to Greco* he himself explains the incident by the fact that he had met and desired a certain woman at a moment when, completely immersed in the Buddhist vision, he was also leading his own war against desire with dubious consequences for his health.

This unexplainable disease inspired in him a near Dionysian appreciation for the body, where the whole world enters, meets and is remoulded. Further and further away from Buddha he becomes more and more vulnerable to what is happening around him — demonstrations, conferences, the youth planning to change the foundation of the world, Russia the Promised Land — and at the same time to the new turn in philosophical thought which in the West had started with Nietzsche and was finally to become canalized in existentialism.

A lot has been written about the influence of Buddha, Nietzsche and Bergson on the work of Kazantzakis and particularly on *The Saviors*. He himself often refers to them — as well as to Lenin, Odysseus and Zorba — as the lighthouses of his life. We are not going to go into philosophical comparisons here because we lack both the philosophical training and ultimately the conviction that there can be any substantial results from such an analysis. Besides, *The Saviors* hardly enters the realm of philosophy nor is it the philosophical expression of a credo.

Kazantzakis himself hesitates in putting his work in any defined category, ". . .I am in a hurry to have printed the whole of my work up to now in order to give myself completely to my new, purely theological work."[13] He also says, "I am writing *Spiritual Exercises*, a mystical book wherein I trace a method by which the spirit may rise from cycle to cycle until it reaches the Supreme Contact."[14] Is it theology, cosmology, new psychology, political mythology? Or is it what he later was to say about *The Saviors*: "My ideas on communism you know, and I've formulated them in a difficult but clear way in the *Spiritual Exercises*."?[15] Overflowing with poetry, i.e. metaphors, images and analogies though without being restricted to any poetical form, it is often, as Kazantzakis calls it, a "Cry" and as all cries, when they are articulate enough, it is the expression of an intense, vital need where the word is a means and not an end in itself.

Kazantzakis' Cry is first of all human because it witnesses the realization of the responsibility of man towards the world. Then it is philosophical because it tries to establish a discipline through the word and finally it is religious because it strives to mould the face of a God. *The Saviors* thus aims at a double target. First, to deal with the three basic existential questions: From where, why and how, that is, from where life, why life and how life? Second, to go deeply into the position of a historically concrete individual living in times of radical change when, on the one hand, he is possessed by these existential questions and, on the other, he wants to take an active part in the creation of history and share with the rest of mankind the responsibility for its shaping. For as long as Kazantzakis was in a Buddhic climate the existential anguish was a personal state of being, a vertical relationship with existence and ultimately with the cosmos. Conscience was contemplating the world from outside. Now, *The Saviors* attempts a synthesis between these two concerns, the existential and the historical, *within* the world.

We are aware, of course, that from one point of view there is no such thing as a contemplation of the existential problem outside historicity but here we are examining the proposition from the point of view of Kazantzakis, who felt that he was developing from the closed world of Buddha to the involved world. Thus, through all the stages, steps and developments of a long march, and in spite of an ever-enlarging cycle of vision, *The Saviors* remain *in* the world even in the last chapter "Silence", which was written much later.

Having established this dimension of space, so to speak, we come face to fact with the second dimension of this work, which is God; Kazantzakis' idea of God, the cornerstone of the whole edifice and also the core of the Kazantzakian argument. What is its real essence since in the totality of his work one can find all sorts of opposite and contradictory elements that can lead to the most opposite and contradictory theories? If by spirituality we mean hoping for divine supervision over creation, reward, and the preservation of the personality after death, then Kazantzakis was not spiritual. But if we mean the thirst for an absolute answer to the ever-unanswered questions, then he was.

There is a God in *The Saviors* but there is no hope; there is a believer but no object of belief. This God, who is born from a paradox and lives through a constant contradiction, is the main difficulty of the work but at the same time the key for establishing the second dimension of *The Saviors:* Kazantzakis made his God from *atheistic elements.* To the existential "WHY" *The Saviors* answers from the very beginning: "We come from a dark abyss, we end in a dark abyss, and we call the luminous interval life." We have here the seed of despair similar to the one from which the tree of existentialism will grow. In reality, the absurd can already be felt here if, as Albert Camus says: "The absurd is born of this confrontation between the human need and unreasonable silence of the world."

On the one hand, the incapacity of the mind to conceive the meaning of existence, and on the other, the refusal of man to limit himself within the narrow bounds of the mind, that is, the world of appearances, as well as the complete renunciation of hope, are the basic premises that Kazantzakis requires of the reader who is starting the ascetic march. Here again, the march must not be conceived of in relation to a purpose. There is no purpose. The God of *The Saviors* is not an end but a way. Kazantzakis does not want to reach God but to live inspired by him. He stands thus between the nostalgic rejectors of faith who return to faith from the opposite road, taking darkness, despair and silence as super-logical proofs of the divine light (i.e., the first existentialists such as Kierkegaard and Shestov), and the classical existentialists (i.e., Sartre and Camus) later on, where the existential man has absorbed the mechanism of the absurd so well that he lives *through it* and *from it,* that is, within its limitation and not with the originally supposed freedoms.

In *The Saviors* we have the Nietzschian freedom which consists of the liberation of man from God and from the repressions that centuries of faith have caused him. We have the Nietzschian YES to life. And, above all, we have the Bergsonian "elan vital" (Kazantzakis calls it spirit), the perpetual moving energy of the world which is inconceivable to the mind in so far as it is impossible to express. (In *The Saviors* Kazantzakis calls it verbal immobility, meaning that the word kills movement since, by trying to define it, it immobilizes it). All the above elements, i.e., freedom from purpose, freedom from hope and the conscious participation of the individual in the elan vital, constitute the features of the struggling God of Kazantzakis. He is made in the image of man and is identical to man. Kazantzakis' God does not believe in God. In the letters to Papastephanou and to Galatea, in *The Saviors*, this divinity is defined in basically a negative way: "He is not almighty, he is not all-wise, he is not all-kind." Kazantzakis' God not only has no hope to offer but he himself is in danger. "Help" is the cry man hears in himself. It is the Cry of God that we hear who, bleeding and in agony, makes his way to the surface so that he may again give birth to matter and from matter and its transformation into spirit make it possible for him, too, to be reborn. When Kazantzakis says, "Our duty is to transubstantiate matter into spirit", this transubstantiation has no relation to any return of man to God but signifies man's victory over a non-God.

The question that arises, of course, concerns the utility of such a God who does not abolish the absurd but intensifies it, who is not a comfort but a source of despair and who, by being hardly more eternal than man, speaks not of immortality but of death. Why should Kazantzakis create his God from the same substances, blood and muck, that he himself is made of, why imprison him in the same world of appearances and then expect man to blow life into him? The answer probably lies in the realization that *The Saviors* is not theology but a form of anthropology. From the stage of Preparation to the final Ascent, Kazantzakis offers man the struggle and the way up while constantly reminding him of

the Abyss surrounding the March. Here we would like to
note a basic difference between the absurd man of Camus
(*The Myth of Sisyphus*) and the man of Kazantzakis. "We
have to imagine the first one happy" as he proceeds with his
endeavors along a path where the only real value is life. This
value is a quantitative one since "there will never be any
substitute for twenty years of life and experience" for the
absurd man, and since, from the purely dogmatic,
existentialist point of view, "living is keeping the absurd alive.
Keeping it alive is above all contemplating it."

Kazantzakis' man follows an ascending path. In reality,
he tries to make a synthesis between a courageous
contemplation of chaos (as does Sisyphus) and the
qualitiative dimension of faith. This faith does not
underestimate either man's intellect in the sense that it
refuses the perpetuation of ontological mythologies or man's
unique capacity to live the non-existent. For the justification
of this attempted synthesis — death and ascent, abyss and
God — we must briefly go back to the historical moment
that inspired in Kazantzakis the vision of *The Saviors*. It was
the moment where human conscience began to give up the
effort to grasp the historical necessity behind the absurdity
of the First World War which brought economic, moral and
psychological collapse in its wake. Kazantzakis along with
other reformers felt the urgency of creating new structures
for society and man. On the other hand, centuries of history
and the evidence of so many civilizations showed that man
can be great only when motivated by faith. As he writes in
The Saviors, "But we named it God for only this name, for
primordial reasons, can stir our hearts profoundly."[16] In spite
of the fact that by then man was fully aware of the absurdity
of his existence, he still felt emptied by the absence of any
faith, this great generator of energy. But Lenin had come to
announce a new faith: faith in man and in his right to rule
over his own life, to govern and not be governed. While this
could be the perfect answer for Kazantzakis and while — as

we see in these letters — he is strongly impressed by the new message, it is quite peculiar that it was then, at precisely that time, that *The Saviors*, that is, his own personal vision, was shaped: "I want to find a single justification wherein I may live and bear this dreadful daily spectacle of disease, ugliness, injustice and death."[17] It becomes evident that even though he embraced Marxism with much hope, deep in himself he felt that it did not cover the totality of human anxiety.

The Saviors expresses the conviction of Kazantzakis that only separately can each man in himself fertilize the seed of revolution. It is man's heart that must overcome comfort and sleep. Only man's heart can make the most extreme opposites meet: Knowledge of death and pleasure, faith in the indestructible flow of existence which, nevertheless, is not immortal. Kazantzakis has above all a passion for life and this passion is the essence of his God, "I believe means I create", he writes, and the peculiarity of this creation is that it has both the awareness of the lack of faith and the exaltation of faith; "We fight because we like fighting, we sing even though there is no ear to hear us. We work even though there is no master to pay us our wages when night falls. We do not work for others, we are the masters. This vineyard of earth is ours, our flesh and blood."[18]

One could not, we think, overlook the prophetic yet somehow immediate character of these letters from a personal and historical point of view. Personally, Kazantzakis expresses his deep desire to serve history in its national and also world course without making concessions, without fanaticism and without betraying his own personal vision. He conveys a feeling of powerlessness of every individual effort or work of art before the chaos of the contemporary world. Like us today, Kazantzakis was also seeking a faith which would liberate energy and not create slavery. Historically, he is crying for a new foundation on which man can put his feet. He already announces the end of small-scale changes in 1922. Fifty years later, the big changes still have not taken place.

And like those who are vigilant today, Kazantzakis does not come down as God to offer solutions either. He merely announces man's duty not to compromise and not to run away: "Die every day. Be born every day. Deny everything everyday. The superior virtue is not to be free but to fight for freedom."[19]

Katerina Anghelaki Rooke
April, 1978

Letters to Papastephanou

LETTER 1

Berlin, 5 September, 1922

Brother Papastephanou,

Seldom have I felt so much emotion as I did from your latest letter. I was deep in the wilderness and I was crying out, bringing the Word to the stones and the waters. I said to myself that our first duty is to cry out in the wilderness. My God! how isolated and desperate, yet how certain I was. The West is rotting and all the beautiful works of art that as recently as last year still moved me deeply and filled my heart, this year seem to me petty, narrow and unworthy of the immense contemporary hope of man.

The pictures and the music are beautiful, the songs are beautiful, Dante and Homer too. The point which man has attained after centuries of effort regarding beauty, thought and action is miraculous. But all this appears to me now like a shed snake skin, like the stereotyped form of a body which itself has moved on, uneasy, naked and trembling in the hostile air, and which is now striving to create its new incarnation.

I roam the streets like Muhammed who ran around smashing all the false gods of the Kaaba with his iron staff. After seven years of preaching he had only eleven disciples, women for the most part. Ah! the day they were expelled the eleven houses were sealed up and they went into exile. God, when will our persecution begin. But first the preaching must begin. I think I'll die of anguish. I still haven't the strength to begin. My mind is completely mobilized but I can't make the terrible leap. I am fighting here, I am laying siege to the critical moment. I felt ill. Now I have recovered and I am continuing the struggle. I plan to finish the *Symposio*, a book in which I write comments on our Religion, our Creed and our Decalogue. We (you, Lefteris, Sfakianos, Sikelianos and two women) are discussing God around a table. The way Plato talked about love, we talk about God. That's why I beseech you to write me about your theogony in as many details as posssible. In that way you help me a great deal in putting into your mouth exactly the words that suit you. Each one of us will incarnate the new shape of the Struggling One in accordance with his own private soul. I'm writing you, on a separate piece of paper, the provisional formulation of our Decalogue. It would be good if each one of us were to write his Creed — a "Decalogue", a dogma — after having thought over the whole of our religion, and then we'll hold a Council to give it a definite form.

To make things easier I have divided the material as follows:

    1) The essence of divinity (struggling, suffering, joy, hope, etc.)

    2) The relationship between God and man (religion, metaphysics, art).

    3) The relationship between man and man (ethics, philosophy, love).

    4) The relationship between man and nature (experience, science, identity). All is one.

* * *

Are there young people in America who could be organized? * * * Write me long and frequent letters. If I'm a bit late in answering don't worry. I'm drowning in agony. Your voice from the other end of the ocean saves me.

N.

LICHTERFELDE WEST
UNTER DEN EICHEN
BERLIN

LETTER 3

Berlin, 10-10-22

Son of Thunder!

You make my heart flame, your voice is like a waterfall. If you were standing next to Christ you would be the Son of Thunder.

I visualize you at the other end of the ocean and my heart feels stronger. I overcome time and place and become one with you. I have never been so much with you because I have never been so far away from the Gehenna of individualism. Here in a foreign land I experience Greece so much, its sky and earth, its great mission. The motionless vision of God enfolds me like light. I'm confident for I know that if I lift my head up, if I stretch my arm out, I'll touch huge, invisible wings.

Lord! Lord!

If I raise my eyes I'll see you standing in front of me, smiling at me with your finger on your lips. I hold you, I inhale you and there's no hurry.

With my head back, with my eyes and mouth closed, I rejoice in your descending.

You descend from secret lofty sources like the great river Missouri, heavy, thick, fecund, without haste or roar.

And all the insects are drinking in the dewy air and rejoicing while the calves let go the udder and lower their heads without knowing the reason.

You descend without roar, without haste, red as blood, bubbling like must, heavy with so much creation.

And whatever you touch becomes a mouth that drinks you.

And whatever you don't touch remains fallow, cursed and unsown forever.

Lord! Lord!

Like a palm tree I stood at the side of the road for you to give me water. I'll lift you from my very roots to my top for you to see and rejoice over your work.

And on the highest branch I'll set my heart warbling, with its head turned to the light, warbling like a nightingale that falls to the earth from too much song — and its beak is bloody.

My God, how can I find the words to express such a flood! Only my head floats above the waters, like Noah's Ark, and likewise, it is full of trees, animals and people; all the seeds are inside and are guarded because the curse of death has flooded the earth as high as my neck and has drowned everything. Sometimes, like the ancient hermit, I feel the seams of my skull creaking.

Never has theogony been revealed to me as being so fearful, nothing but patience, wandering and anguish! I can remember, it was I who nearly drowned amid the thick leaves of the tree and the dark loins of the animal and now I have escaped; I breathe the clear air of the human heart and I'm striving to surpass this, too, to go up higher! To breathe surveying the terrible march ahead of me and behind me!

The huge encampment of God is stretching around me. When I close my eyes I feel that my body is the war tent where, for one moment, the great General has stopped and put on his armor!

Yesterday, while leaving the pedagogical conference I met a very young and ardent Russian Jewish poetess. We talked. Suddenly I turned to her and said: "Rachel, God is in our heart crying Help! Can't you hear him?"

She shuddered. Later on she said to me, "Never has a word broken into my heart with such a thrust. For years I've been feeling an anxiety in me and I didn't know where it was coming from. And now all is clear. I can see, in the stone and in the worm, in the water and in the body, God lifts himself up and cries Help! It is as if we had buried a living being. And now we hear him pounding violently on the partitions of our body and crying out!"

Son of Thunder, let us prepare. There are no more than three of us. It doesn't matter. Organize as many souls as you can over there. Work for our purpose. Get ready. An Ecumenical Council must take place in the next two or three years. Write out our theory so that everything is clear in our mind; express our vision in simple words; find a password for the battle. The apostolic marches will start, the struggles and torture. God within us leaps up to escape from man. He perches on our head and dances like a flame. My God, there is no harsher, more mortal and yet more immortal joy. It is his third leap. What agony!

Always, always
N.

LETTER 4

Brother Papastephanou,

I'm still working on *The Saviors of God*. The first part is "The Preparation." It is divided into three sections:

1) *Appearances contain me* and I work within them. The mind and science, in the realm of appearances, enjoy an absolute authority. No power (religion, ethics, art, etc) has the right to interfere. The intellect dominates absolutely. This is the one reality, the scientific one.

2) *Appearances do not contain me.* Another power in me, let's call it knowledge, let's call it heart, cannot be contained. Anxiety, anguish. What then is behind appearances? What is the mystery that gives birth to them

and supports them? Is there any such mystery at all?
The mind cannot answer such questions. But there is
another power in me which asks and cries out. This is the
second stage of preparation.

3) *I feel that behind appearances there is a struggling
essence.* I feel that this essence laboriously ascends a veiled
and endless acclivity. I feel that it is hastily going down a
dark endless declivity. I correlate my rhythm with it. I
ascend, I descend, together with the universe.

In my ephemeral heart two eternal streams meet. I
sense everything in me growing heavy, wanting to fall and
decompose. The mind gets tired, the body decays, I'm short
of breath. The whole earth is like a millstone round my
neck.

But at the same time I'm swept up by the wrath in me,
an agonized determination to fight, not to give in, not to die.

I conceive of the Universe in the same way. I flow with
it. There is no good, there is no evil, everything is
submerged in vanity, everything is sacred. I yield myself, I
suffer and struggle together with all beings.

But suddenly in this dumb faceless flow a cry springs up
in me: Help! From that point Liberation starts.

i. The "March" starts. Who cried out? I feel in my
heart that the ascending stream, the Invisible One going up,
is the one who cried: Help! That's how the flow begins to be
divided and we begin to take upon ourselves the
responsibility of calling one of the two ways up. Which
should we choose? The inclination downward (like Buddha)
or the exaltation upward?

It is the heart that decides, without intellectual
arguments, following its own special impetus. My heart cries,
"Upward!"

That is how the "March" starts. The stages are: 1) Ego.
2) Race. 3) Humanity. 4) Earth. 5) Universe. At the
beginning of the march my enemy is revealed to be the

world. There is good and evil, enemy and friend, God and
Anti-God. Good is whatever helps the ascent; evil whatever
forces you down. That is how I gradate the values, find my
new Decalogue and regulate my thought and action. As I
advance (coming nearer the Invisible One) I begin to realize
that good and evil co-operate, that not simply "War" but
"Militant Love" is the deepest rhythm of the March.

ii. When I have experienced the whole March then the
great Moment of Union will come. The lover who started off
and fought to arrive, arrives and becomes the bridegroom. It
is the Moment of the Perfect Union with God, the ecstasy. It
is divided into two parts: Ecstasy-fire and Ecstasy-light.

iii. And when we have traced the whole cycle of
preparation, of research and of the mystical marriage, the
great and final stage of Exercise starts: Action.

Then perfectly mature and enlightened we face
appearances, our everyday life, our human duty, that is, the
relationship between God and man, the relationship between
man and man and the relationship between man and nature.

I have sketched for you in a few words the outline of
The Saviors of God. Ah! if only we were together we would
be able to talk about all this. I proceed with toil, trying
through a mysterious and unyielding logic to regulate the fire
of my strength. First of all, we have to clearly establish our
relationship to science. This is the first step. Whoever does
not recognize the omnipotence of science within its cycle
and its impotence outside the realm of appearance cannot
be saved.

If you have any observations to make, write me
immediately. If something is left vague or unanswered in
your mind, write me. If you have learned anything new from
your life there, if you see our God differently, write me
about everything, everything. Our God is the great
Ascender. He seizes hold of all beings so he won't fall. He
seizes our heart and cries out. We dash with him. We

identify our fate with his. Will we be victorious? At the first step, of the initiation we say we will be victorious. The good will be victorious. At the second step we say victory and defeat, good and evil, up and down, beginning and end, matter and spirit are all naive distinctions of the mind. The indestructible struggle is the essence of God. Without end, without reward, and beyond all Purpose. Don't ask. Ascend!

What we say at the third step, I cannot tell you. No one can tell another. Silence.

N.

I wrote you already that Lefteris wants to come here. I told him to come and we'll share whatever I have. It is necessary to be carried away by huge masses of people and ideas so that we can see all the terrible contemporary needs. Our cry must not be idyllic, an aesthetic position, a reply of provincial serenity. There where you are, try as hard as you can to see and experience the wretchedness of today, the excitement, the dishonesty and the longing for Liberation. For someday we must correlate ourselves perfectly with life. To experience profoundly the third stage of "Preparation." Then it will be necessary for us to meet. Then everyone will have written his own *Saviors of God*, that is, his method of liberation, how he lives it and the way he thinks about it so it will be comprehended by others. Lefteris writes, you and I write, we're working. Our life is sacred, our duty is to be careful in every action and thought of ours, to laugh and cry, to work, to love and to always have the great Mandate in front of us.

N.

LETTER 5

Brother Papastephanou,

After so many months I received your brilliant letter, thank God. Where should I begin? Ah! In letters, from afar like this, it is impossible to communicate anything. It requires gesture, voice, silence, laughter, paleness, the contact of the hand, all the warm and mysterious air that circulates between two people talking and struggling.

On the highest level, it is "Silence". And I don't mean Silence the way you do. It is not extreme despair, it is not annihilating or incurable ignorance. Silence means that anyone who has passed through the two levels and has ended his involvement in all contests reaches the highest peak of his Self, beyond every contest, beyond all content, beyond purpose, certainty, joy and hope. All these struggles are the contests that come before, which he passed through and which he no longer needs. He no longer asks, no longer struggles, no longer divides; he matures wholly, silently, indestructibly and inflexibly with the Universe. He adapts himself and infuses the Abyss just as the seed of Man does the womb of Woman. From now on, the Abyss is his wife, he plows her, opens her, he devastates her vitals, he transmutes her blood, he shakes, laughs, cries, ascends and descends with her and he never leaves her!

How can you reach the womb of the Abyss and fertilize it? This cannot be said, it cannot be communicated with words; each one has his own personal way. It is absolutely free; there is no instruction, there is no deliverer to open the way. Each one ascends by his own personal mind to escape time and place.

However, we are compelled to speak. What you feel in ecstasy you'll never be able to say. But you can struggle unceasingly to say it. Struggle to express it through myths, metaphors, allegories, images, rare words, cries and laughter. God, the Great Ecstatic, does the same. He speaks, struggles to speak with incitement, using plants and animals, men, ideas, wings, colors, horns, claws, leaves, fruit, as much as he is able to, in order to stabilize his ecstasy. We are the same and it is our duty to follow his method.

No! No! God is not what you described to me, that is, man and his love of the spiritual, the absolutely beautiful. God is something much deeper which contains all that and its opposite, and who hates all of it and leaves it behind him for the naive, simple souls who are left on the way. If we say that God is an *erotic wind that crushes bodies in order to pass on* and if we think that individuals are always destroyed in blood and tears and that Love still works, then we draw a little nearer to his terrible face.

I wrote to you before that God for me is the Struggler, in every moment, in every body, struggling to rise upward and bridge the gulf between matter and soul. He cries out, he lifts himself a bit and with difficulty breathes through the plants but cannot and begins to suffocate. He leaps, gasps, he wants to speak through animals but his cry is inarticulate, unstable, all hunger and anger. He struggles and crawls between their bodies leaving in them all the passion and darkness he can, and creates and takes hold of man. It is our turn. He plows us, struggling with our bodies, with our brains, continually wanting to escape. How? There are two great exists, those of Love and Death. He urges us on and we transmit the spark of Life — his life — from son to son, always begging the son to surpass the father. He molds, crushes, remolds, trains himself. We work not for ourselves, nor for the humanity of the sociologists and philosophers. We work for Someone Else, who is inside us, who is always moving upward, who has not pity, who has no concern for animals or men, nor for ideas or feelings; all these are his weapons, his ammunition and food — but he tramps on them and ascends.

This is God. Whoever is able, let him lift his head and look him in the face.

I and my God are not two friends; he is not the father and I the son. He is not the master and I the slave. Our love is rough, we sit at the same table and drink the same wine in this low tavern of the earth. And as we clink our glasses, we hear the sounds of swords, of hate, of love; we get drunk; visions of slaughter rise up before our eyes, towns are destroyed within our minds. Both of us are wounded and screaming from the pain as we raid a large Palace.

And sometimes as horsemen, like two knights, we travel under the burning sun or through light rain and we chat, pale and hungry; we are cold and we seal our lips, unyielding. "Leader." "Comrade." He turns his face to me and I shudder to see his agony and his pallor.

Thus we move on, thus we proceed, without reward, without rest, without certainty, I and my God. Whoever can is welcome to follow us.

Here I am writing you thus, hurriedly, about our struggle again. Be careful, avoid constructing the face of our God from what you have learned of the God of the Christians. Our God is not all-good, all-beautiful, all-wise. If he were, what value would our co-operation have? If he were, how would we be able to suffer, struggle and ascend? Avoid romantic theology, human hopes, the certainties that the cowards, both optimists and pessimists, have always had. There is nothing certain in the Universe. We launch ourselves into Uncertainty, we play with our fate every moment, we have influence over whether the Universe will be lost or saved. We have enormous responsibility. For neither destruction nor salvation is certain. We fight together with one of the two currents and we will see which one wins.

N.

So. Now I'm again agitated by the desire to travel; maybe this winter I'll go to India. I have finished *Buddha* and I would like to breathe the air and see the light of India before giving it its final form. Perhaps I will now write another book call *Seven Discussions*.[1]

Here I've found a nucleus of Jews, and I'm offering them communion with our God. They are the only race that can accept him. In Greece there are only two or three souls. No more. And many Russians, both men and women. I'm preparing for a trip to Russia next year. The need for a heart to heart talk with many people is consuming me. What is all this you are saying about my life? What meaning does it have? And what do you mean? To keep the Word hidden just from fear? And even if we wanted to, the Word could not be kept hidden.

God be with you!
N.

∽∾∽∾∽

LETTER 6

Berlin 1922-23

Brother Papastephanou,

I've begun a new book, completely mystical:
SALVATORES DEI
Its purpose is to teach the method of deliverance through simple and brief words. It is divided into four parts with a continually broadening scope:

1) The exit from the Ego. 2) The exit from Humanity and the Earth. 3) The exit from the Universe. 4) The exit from the Exit.

Each cycle has its commandments, its exercises, its merits. From the highest cycle the supremely initiated descend to everyday life and get involved with men, they live, they work, they marry, but in a completely different light.

The starting point of deliverance is the Cry. Here is a page about that:

1. The entire heart of man is one Cry. Lean your head to your breast and listen to it. Someone in you is struggling and crying out.

2. It is your duty, at every moment, day and night, in joy and in grief and within the needs of daily life, to distinguish this cry.

3. Distinguish this cry violently, yet with restraint, according to your nature, acting and thinking, and fight to learn who is crying out.

4. And what he wants.

5. And how we will be able to organize ourselves and save him.

6. In the midst of our greatest joy, someone inside us cries out: "I'm suffering! I want to escape from your joy! I'm hiding!".

7. In the midst of our greatest despair someone inside us cries out: I don't despair, I struggle! I'm hooked in the top of your head, I unsheathe myself from your body, I unsheathe myself from the earth.

8. "I don't fit in brains, in names, in deeds!"

9. Within our strictest sense of virtue someone rises up and despairingly cries out:

10. "Virtue is narrow, I can't breath. Paradise is small and narrow, it won't hold me!

11. Your God looks like a man to me; I don't want him!"

I am preparing lectures; I am already speaking with Russians, and Jews from Russia and Poland, who have accepted our religion with ardor and changed their life. They were ready for it. With them, I talk, laugh and live; I breathe as I never did in Greece. I feel you there far away, also struggling and crying out. Lefteris is doing the same in Crete. We must, without fail, found churches in various places. I gave a book to a Jewess here and I wrote, "Rachel, God is in your heart and he's crying: Save me!" I wrote it just like that, as a test, and as soon as she read the sentence she jumped up and her eyes filled with tears. Ever since, she has been our most fervent disciple. I'm impatient to finish *The Saviors of God* and to send it to you so that you can make your remarks and so that all three of us agree completely before I send it to be translated (in Hebrew and Russian for a start) and before it is printed and distributed secretly to the converts.

Thus, here in a foreign land far from Greece, far from Venizelos, Kings, friends, social calls, far from vain chatter, I work on and strengthen the features of our God. But as soon as I can I'll leave for Russia. If I only knew Russian! If only I had your ardor, your divine exaltation! I feel that I could then proclaim a new crusade against modern civilization, and together with millions of hungry, holy Russians, flood Europe. That is what I could do. The world has gone rotten, O, Lord! We have to plant a new one. Never has the earth been more deeply, more painfully tilled than today. Everything is ready, what's missing? The seed! I feel I hold the seed in my hands, as if it were a hand grenade. If only I could jump over the fence of logic and throw it into the human fields.

My God is all mud, blood, desire and vision. He is not pure, immaculate, almighty, all-wise, just and all-kind. He is not light. Through agony and toil, night in his bowels is transubstantiated into light. He climbs, panting, the slope of virtue. He's crying out for help. He doesn't save us. We save him. SALVATORES DEI! What does it mean, that we save him? We save the eternal breath in our ephemeral clay existence; we transform flesh, air and water into spirit.

Within the workshop of the body we construct spirit from matter; we free God. Our life has no other purpose. Overcome fear! Overcome virtue! For what? Towards what? Don't ask. Fight! Get behind appearances, mix with the eternally struggling essence. This earth is good, this body is good, matter is sacred, all saintly, for these can become spirit through our love and through our struggles. Only at the first stage of initiation is there good and evil. At the second stage, good and evil work together. Don't forget that. Two strong, opposite winds, one masculine and one feminine, met and clashed at a crossroad. This crossroad is the Universe, this crossroad is my heart. A dance of the five senses, that is what my heart is. A dance of existence, of my five senses, that is what my heart is. Love and war and their supreme synthesis is the purpose of our life.

My dear, no one is vigilant like you, no one burns with your flame. Fight there where you are, as hard as you can, to stir up souls. Make those who are complacent, uneasy; show the happy that they are sunk in the mire of wretchedness. Wake everyone you can. Found an order, convince them in simple words of 1) the essence of our God (pain-joy-hope), 2) the relationship between God and man (as between the soldier and the General), 3) the relationship between man and man (allies — each one undertakes to defend a section of the battle) and 4) the relationship between man and nature (plants, animals — stations where God pitched camp for a moment. Now he has made his camp in Man. But he is in a hurry, he wants to escape, that is why he cries out for help!)

This society of believers must have a stable point of contact with reality. A defined position in the political, social, ethical and economic relationships of man. The simple idea does not suffice; it must be tied to everyday life. Men get confused when far from the soil. Let's give them support!

One, two or three people are enough. I will found the

first churches in Berlin and Poland — all Jews. I'm the only Greek. Not Greek. Cretan.

Write me, write me. Never have you been so close to me, never has distance been so decisively defeated.

God be with you

N.

ᴧᴑᴚᴑᴧᴑᴧ

LETTER 7

1-4-23

Brother Papastephanou,

I received your letter and wrote immediately to Athens, telling them to type up a copy of a tragedy of mine, *Nikiforos Fokas*, and to send it to you. I have another tragedy with me, *Christ*,[1] but I'm not sending it because 1) it is very long, 5,000-6,000 lines and 2) it is somewhat difficult for America.

And here too, in Berlin, the flower of materialistic civilization is enormous, marvelous and horrible — all that you wrote me about also exists here in this small group of men, ascetics, who are struggling against the current and are readying future humanity through convulsions of pain. I know several of them and I admire not so much their loftiness of mind as their organization, insistence and systematic effort. Lectures, public discussions, dances, music etc. They use everything to communicate the light which burns in them.

We don't have to take the content of their ideas from them. Our own content is higher and broader. But we do have to take their method of work. If we stay the way we are now, we will be lost. One cries out in America, one in Greece and one in between. There are some others crying out and we don't hear them; thus our life, not our zeal, is exhausted in "private outcries."

This must not go on. What do you have to say? Try as hard as you can to express it clearly, simply and with few words. Print it, speak it, circulate it. It is not perfect yet. So much the better! It will become perfect when you toss it into the market place and it comes into contact with living souls, warm bodies and open air. Our life passes, we have already passed through the first half of life, we are now at the highest, ripest, most fertile point of the human pyramid. What are we waiting for? We have no right to hate nor love nor indict our contemporaries as long as we dissipate ourselves in murmuring insignificant instruction to the masses.

I'm the number one culprit. I work, write, I have *The Saviors of God* ready, that is, the introduction to our religion; but what does it mean? I must leap into the market place, speak to groups of people and overcome fear.

Since I have seen the entire cycle of the uniqueness of life and death, of good and evil, and at a distance have lived through all the attempts of God to save himself, through matter, through plant, through animal and now through man, my duty is to adapt all this lofty theory to my epoch and to my everyday life.

I now feel more and more that the highest form of the idea is the act. This is the first fruit of the entire divine tree. Therefore, illuminated by my lofty inspection of the struggle of God, I must see what this epoch in which I was born is, and how, within this epoch, I can help God as much as I can in his ascent. What the duty of man was in past epochs (*duty*, that is, *what form man's aid to God took*) and what his duty will be in the future, is not important. What my duty is in an epoch now exhausted, an epoch crying out while giving birth to a new world, that is the only duty I care for. Whether God at some time (for such were the conditions of life, of his development, of the races, etc. etc.) assumed the face of Dionysus or Christ or Zarathustra or Moses or Buddha is today only of historical value. What interests me is his present-day face, full of blood and tears and individual duty. Every day the face of my God becomes more fixed as the strict all-commanding and agonized face of a General in the contemporary and crucial battle between the eternal opposing powers. And, more particularly, my God today is the leader of the masses, dark crowds struggling to free themselves from bourgeois wretchedness and injustice, to breathe freely. What does that mean? That my God is struggling to breathe freely within today's most God-bearing strata (the masses of the people). Previously my God had to save himself from beasts and physical forces, so he took on the form of the king and the aristocrat and created great civilizations. Then he took the face of the bourgeoisie and created great works. Now his old allies have lost their drive, their nobility and their creative spirit — they have become hindrances. And my God is seized by the class that suffers and wants and is able to bear children. And he will leave this one too, as he did the others, when it becomes a hindrance.

"Burn your house," my God cries out. "I'm coming. He who has a house cannot receive me. Burn your ideas, crush your thoughts. I'm coming. He who has found the solution cannot find me!"

"I love the starved, the restless, the vagrant. For centuries they have brooded on rebellion, hunger and the endless way — ME!"

I'm coming. Leave your wife and your children, leave your ideas and follow me. I am the Great Vagabond!"

"Follow me! Stride over joy and grief, over peace and justice and virtue. Forward. Smash these idols, smash them all, they cannot contain me! Smash yourself that I may pass."

"What is your conviction? You must say: 'To unsheathe myself and ascend above every conviction. I'm the traitor and the lover. I betray whatever I love because I'm a believer in the essence of love'."

"And what is the essence of love? You must say: 'Amid ideas and bodies I want to mix with the Invisible'."

I have again written you a few phrases from *The Saviors of God*. Ah! I can't describe how I suffer. I suffer because I can't defeat the absurd and am afraid because I can't loosen the cry from my throat and cry out. However, I am struggling. This is my last labor.

Write me regularly, try to set aside time to fix your ideas on paper. Prepare your lectures, try and speak "indirectly" in church about our God. You could give Christ no greater joy than by preparing for the coming of the Holy Ghost within his churches.

Always.
N.

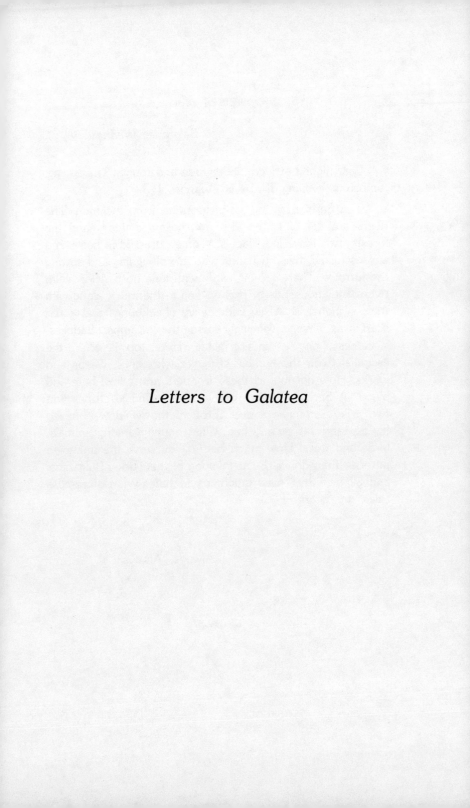

Letters to Galatea

LETTER 11

Belgrade, Wednesday. . .

Last night I arrived in Belgrade and tonight I'm leaving; tomorrow evening I'll be in Vienna.

The Serbian spring looks beautiful from the train. The rivers are full of water lilies and yellow daffodils and the forests with flowering acacias. Women dressed in heavy red aprons follow their husbands who are ploughing and sowing the furrows. There are big cattle with long horns, slow calm rivers and thousands of pigs wading in the muck along with their swineherds. A girl with heavy cheekbones and a red scarf was singing longingly over the swamps. Sadness, sweetness, pity — indescribable. Here too is Man, the essential man, the humble struggler who sings, weeps and works. How horrible all these frontiers are, full of hate and blood. A Serbian beetle, with enormous indigo stripes and two silky antennae came through the window, buzzed happily and sat on my hat. What a unity among animals, birds and trees! How much better they serve the unknown purpose than do men. I'm thinking of the Turks, Bulgarians and all men that have taught us to hate. What sweetness rules my heart!

* * *

Always, Always
N.

LETTER 13

Sunday, 21 May, 1921

I hope to find a pension today. Regardless of that, dreadful sights move my heart. The horror of Vienna disintegrating is beyond description. A special police service has been organized to keep people from throwing themselves into the Danube at night. But many escape the attention of the police and throw themselves in, especially mothers with their children. At night thousands of women circulate in the street and offer themselves for a bite to eat. Starving sex! There's no sorrow more terrible! 800,000 people took part in a demonstration the other day. We will soon have a revolution here; France is to blame for this entire catastrophe: It won't allow Vienna with its small *hinterland* to unite with Germany and thus be saved, nor will it allow the holders of capital to make loans to it. Today, before the eyes of a dishonest Europe, millions of women and children are dying of hunger. I read a very beautiful letter from a German writer to a Frenchman which appeared in the *Freie Presse*. I have kept the clipping, to translate it for you. Very bitter, severe, and proud.

"Don't write sentimentalities" he says to his French friend and old classmate. "Whatever you have to say, say it clearly, write your indignation to the newspapers. Friendly, private letters are not enough anymore. You too are responsible for the crimes of humanity as you do not cry out. Cry out, leave the correspondence alone! Put your shoulder next to mine and push with me!"

* * *

My God, how I think about you, and how tragic my life seems to me. I am, as Buddha says, *il sempre alzato*. Always upright, always starting anew.

I go to concerts and museums. This year there is a peculiar change in me. Art seems a luxury to me.

I'm waiting for a letter from you at the Alserstrasse address. Greetings to the troupe.[1] Always, always,

N.

LETTER 15

IX Vienna, Alser Str. 26¹, June 7

Cherie,[1] I felt so much joy on getting your letters again. If you only knew how I welcomed your first letter today. My God, what a joy! You made all my sorrow disappear. I was lying on a chaise longue with my face covered with bandages, holding an ice pack on my forehead, for the eczema has left the area around my lips and chin and has gone up around my eyes and forehead. It had been weeks since I had been out, and just the other day, when I hoped I had done with it, I went to a lecture of the famous theosopher Steiner (at this moment there is a large theosophical conference in Vienna). But when I came back home my eyes were swollen; I called the doctor again; he said it's nothing, I merely have to rest, use ice, etc.

Your letter gave me deep joy in my illness. Here nobody looks after me and I alone (with a clumsiness you can't imagine) put the bandages on, get up by myself day or night to put on fresh salve and so forth. But I'm not nervous about it. I'm calmly waiting until this small trial is over and meanwhile I'm reading whatever I can. I found a man who put me in contact with the communists here; they replied that they must test me first and that their secretary will come to talk to me for this purpose. I hope to see the overthrow here very soon. You simply cannot imagine the intensity the horror has reached. Hunger and infamy, as well as all sorts of depraved characters, have gathered from all ends of the earth, disgracefully enjoying themselves with incredible cynicism. A lot is happening in music, dance and painting; at the same time there are mass meetings by young factory workers, both men and women. The other day they passed under my windows singing the hymn of the proletariat.

In Bulgaria there is a lot going on. I'm sending you a newspaper clipping to have it translated by Mrs. Ladas.[2] But we in Greece are a drained generation, one which will shuffle along, though, in the great dance. It seems that Lenin is dying and that Trotsky, who will succeed him, will be very fierce; he'll split skulls open in order to stick Deliverance in.

* * *

June 11

Little by little and with difficulty I get better. You don't know how much patience I have to exert to put up with all this misfortune by myself and not to get nervous about it. Luckily, I'm much better today. The swelling on my face has gone down. I hope I'll be able to go out in a few days. And only then will I send you this letter so that you will be completely relieved. As for now, I'm glad you weren't here to see me because I was totally disfigured and I would have been ashamed.

Life here becomes more and more ferocious. In a matter of two days everything became twice as expensive because the crown was devalued. When I arrived here, the English pound was 41,000 crowns and now it is 72,000. And it's still going up. They printed 300 billion new crowns so you can imagine what's going on! The locals here can't live anymore. Revolution is coming. Just now, a famous communist that I met here, Jewish of course, came to my room. He is delighted. "The knife has reached the bone, people will start dying in heaps, deliverance is coming. The Revolution!"

I hope I won't leave Vienna before my eyes see this great day. It's true that writing can only have value as a slogan, to fire the hearts, to focus anxiety and to make brothers recognize each other. It is John the Baptist appearing in the desert. And behind him comes the Redeemer with his broadsword. And here I sit and write trying to justify my existence. There are words that are as ripe as actions. If only we find these words so that our struggle won't die, so that our soul won't be snuffed out along with our miserable body.

* * *

I love you
N.

LETTER 17

Cherie, I have just sent you a letter about our financial situation. Now let's chat for a bit. All these days I've been locked up in the house I've been giving the final form to my prose piece, "A Year of Loneliness"[1]. It's written with passion, sometimes very strong but, I think, always with emotion. It still shows my shortcomings[2] but I hope that I'm purifying myself constantly. During these days of my convalescence I take walks by myself in the beautiful gardens here; I saw some multi-colored waterlilies in the ponds today and also some lindens that had just started blossoming. Suddenly I saw a man who looked incredibly like Dostoyevsky. The spitting image, same beard, same glance, same gait. The masks of Luxemburg, Gorki and Lenin that I ordered for you have not come yet. In the meantime you might come and you will be able to get them. Here we are advancing toward an inevitable conclusion, unless the union between Vienna and Germany takes place, in which case liberation will be postponed.[3] Now that I have recovered I will get into close contact with the communists. I wrote to Danilidis[4] to see if there is a chance of starting a communist periodical here and in Berlin and sending it to Greece but I haven't had an answer yet; he may have moved. About five or six years before 1821 *Logios Ermis* was started here in Vienna by Anthimos Gazis, and this magazine prepared the national awakening of Greece; I wish that here again we could start the next great awakening, the human one! Always, when I hope for a tragic continuation of our lives, for an involvement in the Deed, I see you as I saw you — remember? — in that dream of mine. I am deeply moved that fate has allowed me to walk with you on this small, ephemeral path of life. We set off from a dark point, we go to a dark point, and in the half-lit space between we discern the face of the other one, honest, clear, good, and feel comforted. Maybe it is because of my disease that my soul is filled with heroic bitterness. I now understand the heroes who work amid so much physical wretchedness. Bitterness, but because of pride not generalizing one's bitterness — rather, going to the other extreme and appealing to joy and health as a universal law. I was never so ready for a brave act as during the days when the sight of myself, swollen, horrible, with two small holes which just let the glance emerge, filled me with disgust. God, let us not die before we are given the opportunity to prove that we are capable of turning all this we say into action. Maybe when the critical moment comes, we'll turn out to be better than we thought, maybe worse.

* * *

N.

LETTER 19

June 28

Cherie, we are going through critical days suffused with a silent disciplined fever. I wrote you that a general strike broke out a few days ago, covering post office, telephone, telegraph and trains. The Government gave into all except the trains. So the train workers are continuing their strike. Yesterday there was a general tram strike. Just now, as I was writing you, the employees of the trams went by in rows of four, silent, going all around Vienna. No shouts, no speeches, nothing. As soldiers in rows of four with a rhythmical step that echoes in the motionless city like the advance guard of an army that is approaching.

The other day Rathenau was killed. I don't know if I have ever talked to you about my love and admiration for this greatest of all modern writers in Germany. I have some books by him at home and I gave one to Anghelakis[1] to translate but the office and petroleum take up all his time. There is great ferment here, soon we will have destruction and resurrection. How disgusted I was with the letter of Navsika[2] where with passionate words she spoke of spring in Agoriani and her joy in waiting for Anghelos.[3] These small souls still live an idyll, ruminating on their everlasting mush of flowering meadows, swallows building their nests on thyme and fir trees. God, if only they could come here and see the great, the true, the saintly spring. We have no swallows, but we have cripples at every corner of the street begging and singing to attract attention; we have children who gather before the entrances of the big hotels and who, as soon as the gate opens, rush under the tables and collect crumbs. And next to this we have the shameless rich, the Gypsy music, the dance called the shimmy, the night clubs and the men fat and florid from all their steak and lust. God doesn't float down with wild flowers and swallows here; he is heavy, covered with wounds and he cries out!

Who knows when this voice of mine will reach you. We've been cut off from the world. I'm anxious to arrange things with Danilidis about the magazine; the greatest difficulty will be to be allowed to circulate it in Greece. We'll see. Vendiris[4] wrote to me from Munich; he, too, is all in an uproar. We'll have to get together, he says, to talk and work. He'll stay in Germany and he'll come here too; anyway, I'll see him soon.

* * *

N.

LETTER 23

Cherie, it's been days since I had a letter from you. What torture! More and more I feel that I have no greater joy. I'm sad again, I got sick again, got better, I don't know what's wrong with me. I've been to all the doctors and only the one I wrote to you about, the university professor, is right, I think: It is a psychic disturbance which is manifested in the body. Of a kind, he says, with the wounds of St. Francis. He told me that I have a *surnormale* psychic activity and that the body is reacting to this. It may, however, suddenly go away forever. Thus I stay at home for weeks at a time and struggle to work as much as I can so that I won't have the time to worry. But sometimes, in the evening, at twilight, I can't hold back the tears. But I pull myself together again . . . It's a great consolation to me to think that if you were here I would have warm protection. And that does me a lot of good, even if I don't have it. It's enough that I could have it. Now, today, I'm completely cured again.

From today the situation in Vienna has become dangerous for the middle class. The prices have tripled in one month because the pound has risen to 170,000 crowns (when I arrived it was 42,000). People can't get by anymore. Today there was a big demonstration, thousands of people. Red flags were waving and immediately all the shops closed, coffeehouses emptied, people hid. They didn't break any shop windows today. We'll see tomorrow.

Summer is chilly here. Rain all the time. I can't go without a jacket in the house. The gardens are marvelous. There are no trees in the world more beautiful.

I would like you to write me definitely when you're coming so that I can arrange my stay here. I'm thinking of leaving for Germany in August. If you come I'll wait for you and we'll leave together. Together we'll see Munich (only an hour away from Vendiris, who is expecting us), Nuremberg, Weimar, Dresden, Leipzig, Berlin. You'll see fantastic things, so many that you will not be bored with me perhaps, while you are noticing all those beautiful things.

* * *

Cherie, one more word. I don't know how to tell you — because I'm shy — that I have never loved you so deeply, so desperately, as I do now. You tell me that I'm too far away from you. I have nobody but you in the world. You are the only individual existence that moves me to death. I love, as I say, all humans — and what's more, and for the same reason, all animals, trees and stars equally as I do humans. I feel that they are all co-combatants in a sacred procession which starts from a dark point and goes to another dark point.

And nobody knows why, nor what is the importance of all this tumult or if the procession is nuptial or funereal. But I sometimes raise myself above this sea of vanity and throw a silent desperate glance at the blind flood of organisms. I cannot make out any face — they are all drowned in the yellow light of vanity. I cannot distinguish father or sister or friends, not even myself. I can only distinguish You and I would like to make this whole vain, wretched, incomprehensible moment, immortal. I would like to see your face always, so the power, the life and the love in your face would never disappear from before me. You are the only holy face in the midst of God's chaos. I don't know how to say tender things, I don't know how to talk to you so that you will feel, for one moment, how much I love you.

N.

LETTER 29

18 August

Comrade!

Just now on returning home I found your letter. (I had already sent you a letter and a card). I'm completely well, don't worry. I wasn't complaining that I was alone; I just said that I was consoled by the thought that if you were here you would look after me and make the days of my illness more tolerable. I leave, I travel but not on pleasure trips, you realize that. I have terrible agonies in me. I feel I'll die if I stay too long in the same place. I have to change places and get a little outside of myself to forget the terrible mission I gave myself which I can't carry out. However, I'm fighting to carry it out. Isn't that a victory too? A poor one but who knows? I always hope. The things I want are the kind you laugh at, because your mind is well-balanced. And I myself often laugh at these things because I can't overcome reason. When I stop laughing at them then my victory will be complete. God, how frightened I am that I may be of the stuff of Nietzsche. We'll see. I hope I don't have his diseases. This was a completely harmless one as I wrote you but very annoying. It was from worry. For months I haven't talked or laughed. In Berlin, I'll be all right. Besides, I'll be terribly busy with the series of books for Dimitrakos[1] that I have undertaken to handle, and with those that I'm preparing now, and also with the communist magazine and the seven stories for Dimitrakos and my own creative work as well.

* * *

N.

ๅแผผ

LETTER 32

9 September

This very moment I received your letter from Heraklion. I'm so sorry that you didn't have a good time! And I thought that you would be comforted to see, from your new viewpoint, the old framework of our lives — the country roads, the sea, the Venetian walls, even the people — to see them the way we have placed them now, without illusions, without expecting recognition and reward from them but with our fixed and unyielding will to save them, whether they want it or not. It is Man we suffer for, Man we fight for, not for wretched, petty men. I thought that because of the way we see things now, people could not grieve you any longer. Ah! come and stay here for a while when you can. I can't describe how much I love you. I experience deeply what love means and I no longer regret that you deny this capacity in me. But still, when you come you will again have many reasons, and justly so, to call me cruel and insensitive. God, I don't know if you understand my torture!

Horrible news has arrived from Greece. Will the wretched Greeks learn anything now? Will that disaster be the beginning of a renaissance? That's how I take it and I accept it with gratitude. The victory of the present regime would be a disaster for Greece. It would give today's crooks a foothold and would anesthetize the people who want exactly that. But now, this great misfortune will either fortify them or sweep them away. Either way is better than the horrible, poor life they are leading today. It was through catastrophe that Russia and Germany were reborn. With its victory, France reached the height of dishonesty because this victory solidified the capitalist regime which governs it. The bitter trial of our Greece today increases our responsibility and makes intense propaganda more necessary.

Write often and a lot. Velmos wrote me that he saw you one day and that he thought you were sad. Ah! my comrade, I could find no peace all day! You don't know how much you are one with me, how much I think about you, how much I would like to be worthy of you. If once in a while you are, justly, ironical about the chimera which eats at me, I am sad because warmth on your part at this point would be no consolation, but the greatest assistance to me in conquering. Your coldness gives arguments to my thought, and thus is nourished the impetus against my chimera. What do I care if I write one or two good lines, if I find a good metaphor and write an acceptable tragedy? All of this seems to me like sin; that's how much I feel that this takes me away from the difficult, unrewarding mission beyond beauty and individuality that I have undertaken. Whatever I write in terms of art seems to me an act of cowardice, sin, a false way because I am afraid to confront the One, the only thing which cries in me and wants to be born. As an excuse I tell myself that all this is preparation, *apprentissage*. But for how long? You have often told me that I am already old and haven't done anything. And I, as an argument, name great men in order to hide the panic that your words give me. Yes, yes, I say it aloud, you are right. I never did, I never will do anything. I will perish while preparing material for someone else. Maybe — and this is the most bitter of all — nobody. I lose myself in searching, in ephemeral works. I spend my soul on petty things. And when I die nobody will guess, from my life or my wretched writings, the incurable, the supreme unheaval of my soul. And what does that mean? Nothing, because individuality has no value whatsoever. But there was something else in me, higher than this wretched ego, broader than myself and I grieve for not being able tô save that. I am nothing — just a sack, as Buddha said, full of tears, blood, filth and sweat. But, I know for sure, there was God's cry in me: Help!

Ah! if only I could express in *Buddha* all that I think about! I think that this work will be the last temptation of art that will lure me. The seams of my skull creak when I think about the wealth, abundance, joy and sorrow I experience in creating it. Never was my soul so mature, so loaded with fruit, so embittered and so hopeful.

* * *

N.

Käthe Kollwitz

There's a woman here, already old (she was born in 1862) who I'm going to meet in a little while. She's the greatest artist. I bought a series of her printed sketches and I'm sorry I can't send them to you because it is forbidden to export books. Never have the contemporary anguish, the hope and the revenge of the masses been expressed with more pain, or more epigrammatically. Here is poverty, revolution and death! I have them on my desk and I deep thinking it's such a pity you can't share my emotion. The upheaval and fermentation that is taking place here in Berlin is incredible. In art they are seeking new ways and are turning to the savage Gods of Mexico and Africa. They seek a new *spontanéité*, direct contact with contemporary needs, the soul of today naked, without ornaments, which are beautiful but belong to a past era, which means they are false. In education, sexual matters, health, new, dangerous and intoxicating points of view are appearing. Still a chaos, but fertile, full of creativity.

Has Sikelianos published anything new? He was supposed to publish "Asklepion" and I can't wait to read it because it's very beautiful. Please send it to me as soon as it's out.

LETTER 37

October 2

* * *

Lately we've had a conference on educational reform here, a series of lectures from 9:00 in the morning till 7:30 in the evening. Only a one hour break for lunch. I've been following them with great interest. One day I'll write to you about their importance. Ah! won't we ever be given the power to overthrow the wretchedness of Greece! Here I'm studying the renaissance in education and I've met the leaders personally. But more about that some other time.

Greetings to the troupe. Especially to Jenny.

I'm worried about your stomach problems. Please write

me about it. Don't forget your diet. Maybe the revolution will give you a little desire to mend the body. Don't tell me that you are dejected, because my sadness becomes inexpressible. Oh, won't you come. When will you come? That would be a great joy; if only you liked living abroad. I'm trying to find a nice house so when you come you'll like it. You'll see here the renaissance of all intellectual life, and how women talk and fight. They are much better than men.

Write me often. I always answer immediately and if you don't get the letters right away it is the fault of the mail.

I love you
N.

As the very few human beings left in Greece maybe we should formulate a protest addressed, not to the civilized world (there is no such thing today), but to the Mandate of Man, concerning the slaughters and infamy of both the Greeks and the Turks in Asia Minor. A brief, simple, compassionate plea. In case it is done, please don't forget to put down my name. It will be one of the very first and most precious documents of the new evolution of man. It will prove to some exceptional thinkers here that the essence of Greece still lives and is setting a courageous example.

We'll publish it translated into two or three languages in our magazine and in other foreign magazines.

LETTER 38

15-10-22

* * *

What you write about the wretchedness of the Greek is horrible and true. But as I wrote you before, don't forget that these people are not Greece. This filthy generation will die and we two or three will work to make the coming one a little better. What you write about the children is a positive and valuable contribution. As I have said before, I would like to write for children. But I don't have your gift of being able to speak with simplicity. Let us do our duty. Let us at least keep Greece clean in our hearts. It was admirable and honest of you not to sign. What the Greeks did in Asia Minor is as horrible as what the Turks did. From now on we are interested in Man without labels. And in Asia Minor Man was dishonored by both the Greeks and Turks.

* * *

Cherie, my beloved wife, I have nobody in the world but you. At this moment my eyes are dim with tears — tears of love, sorrow and pride because God has given me the chance to walk by your side.

Always
N.

LETTER 40

Cherie, thank you very much for your letter and the newspapers. You are right in everything about the revolution. The mob, those many zeros after the unit are starting to shout again, begging for a new master. We have all this misery and all these half-done things because our race is now at a crucial moment of decay. And over all this ephemeral mass, dark and unconscious, the mind of the creator stands out; he alone is enlightened and he contemplates an ephemeral figure (let's say Plastiras)[1] and endows it with immortality. Ah! how deeply I feel your emotion and indignation. Will there ever be a time when we'll be able to live and do something more complete? I begin to acquire certainty. A terrible agony, like labor pains, shakes the world. You in Greece can't feel it. But here, my God, how strongly some people (the Franks, as we used to call them in contempt) struggle to save men. I wrote to you about the conference of the progressive reformers of education. You should have seen the leaders. One, Destereich, stands out. An ascetic, gaunt, about 45 years old, tall, fierce, extremely poor. He wears threadbare clothes of *peau de diable* and when he talks he forgets that he's talking about schools and with vehemence and hate begins to tear apart the structure of this awful contemporary social life. Thousands of young people, blond, ingenuous, real workers, listen to him; some cry, some get organized and from their activities the formidable *Jugendbewegung* (organization of youth, sic) has emanated, which dominates all of Germany. You have to see these young people (the age limit is 35) how they sing, take excursions, work, how they dress, how they think — both boys and girls. It's a new atmosphere, a struggle to liberate not only the German, not only the worker, but Man. A great religious current runs through this organization. They publish books, their own newspapers, they help each other; they are the spiritual army of the future mobilization.

Today, another conference ended, on "Rhythm". Its aim was to show through dancing and movement the various disciplines whose purpose is the education of the body to become an obedient instrument of the contemporary soul. On the basis of the modern movements of the worker, the fisherman, the carpenter, the walker and the dancer, a system of body training has been created which has marvelous results. They say that the love of the body and its education is the basis of the reform of the contemporary soul. So we have here proletarian body training and no longer the classical vomitings of Duncan. Yesterday afternoon, Duncan demonstrated her aristocratic dances and imitations from ancient vases, etc. and was whistled off. "What do we care about this?" the young people yelled, "what relation does it have to our life? We are workers and we don't care about ancient times."

But I may be tiring you and I don't know what Athens will be like when you read this letter. It's true that here the echo of the Greek tumult sounds far away, small, a detail. The winter that has just started here is tragic. The misfortune and the organized indignation of Germany is beyond description.

* * *

Always
N.

LETTER 41

Cherie, I'll answer your letter immediately. What you wrote me is true. I know that I'm not doing my duty perfectly, that I sit here in solitude and like the famous patriot cry out the well-known phrase: "Either all of you will die, or we all shall be free." All the things you say I've thought about myself and my only answer is that I am not a complete man as yet. I say "as yet" not because of cowardice but because I'm struggling to overcome my weakness. I'm good at finding what's right, at setting fire to some souls, at inflaming some brains, but I cannot by myself make contact with men, nor fight against indifference, ridicule and everyday small talk. If I go back to Greece I don't think that I will be ready to throw myself into the fight immediately. I'll go and isolate myself in the country again, receive some select people and talk with them on Sundays.

And what else? I have not yet managed to overcome Art. I'm still mortally seduced by beauty, the good image, the faithful metaphor, the tragic vision of life expressed in words. I say that even if a State perishes (especially a wretched one like Greece) it is of no importance. First of all because maybe only then will a bright, witty, and adaptable race be freed. And then because that's how the world is whether we like it or not. The political forms which give birth to hate must disappear. And if the Greeks disappear because they are unworthy, then blessed be the hour of their disappearance. They'll empty this splendid corner by the sea that they infect and other men will come to honor Man's name.

I don't know if it's for good or bad that I have escaped from the border of the Greek homeland. Yes, I belong to the Greek race and its fall is also my fall — because the elements that it gives me, with which and only with which I can work here on this earth, are decadent. But I'll repeat that I feel that our Cretan race is not Greek. Cretans are also terrible, of course, but it's because they are under the sway of the Greek wretchedness. Deep in themselves they are healthy, barbarous, pure and creative. I'm struggling to escape. All I've written up to now (as well as *Buddha*[1] which I'm writing now) are the visible traces of my struggle to escape from concern, weakness and the unnecessary luxury of my imagination. In *Buddha* I leave behind a great many of my imperfections. Maybe when I'm finished writing it and am relieved of the poetic images which weigh on me, I'll be able to do my duty; I'll be able to submerge myself in contemporary restlessness and hope and to work, no longer with words but with people. But even then I doubt if I'll go back, to proclaim the solution which I think will save the contemporary soul, to the Greeks. Lefteris[2] wrote me about the day he tried to explain our ideas to Avgeris,[3] Varnalis[4] and Company. Only you, in your contempt for the insensitive and the faithless, got up and defended us. The others were laughing and tossing around insults while Sfakianakis[5] was spinelessly silent. What does this mean? That I'll find difficulties in Greece? Not only that; my duty then would be to fight, to overcome the difficulties. It is something more; the Greeks are still completely unprepared to listen to an idea and be stirred. They are petty shopkeepers, insignificant schoolteachers and cowards. I don't know if there are three like you in the whole Greek race — those who will stand up and honor an idea even if they do not agree completely.

I'm thinking a lot about going to Russia. Ah! if only we were Russians. Here is a people that needs the Idea more than bread. All the seeds of the future boil and dance in its famished, devastated innards. Even the humblest Russian souls, the emigres here, have filled Germany with their women, music, dance, painting, with their cabarets and songs; what exalted souls, what dizzying heights!! All for all!

I don't know how I will go to Russia, how I will have any effect, how I will talk to the people. Sometimes epic visions, mad visions, fill my mind. The idea is boiling in me that Russia will set off on a crusade with the new God and trample down Europe. The new proletarian God will crush the horrid and infamous political, economic, moral and spiritual idols and proclaim a new freedom to the world. All Asia is in turmoil, crucified Russia is expectant and waiting for the Resurrection. Europe is being ever more deeply submerged in infamy and darkness. I don't know how this earthquake appears in Greece, but here the chaos is visible and tangible and the struggle for a new order most deep.

It's Man I think about, Man — whether he be Turk, Greek, Jew or whatever. We must save him. Should we start with Greece? I don't think so; that we would perish is of no importance but our Word would also perish, and this is unjust. Many times the Word has perished, falling on barren stones. But because we are now following the steps of God on this earth in full consciousness, we don't have the right to walk for nothing.

Ah! we should be together and talk. Nothing can be done through letters. You'll have objections to whatever I write and I can't hear them and answer immediately. I'm flooded with words and I no longer know how to write to you in a way that my answer will seem logical. Write me, answer me, since we have no other means of communication. I sit here and cry out to you. God, how many days will go by before you hear me?

Always, always

N.

~~~

LETTER 43
(written in pencil)

Cherie, I'm sending you this card of Kokoschka because I felt such a joy when I saw this painting the other day, and I wanted to communicate some of it to you. Its beauty is indescribable. The Russians now have their own painting exhibition here. What passion, what joy, what new directions! There is a Russian ballet here as well as a Russian musical group and a Russian cabaret — an invasion by the Slavic soul, a conquering of Europe. Through the terrible misfortune of present-day Russia the Russian soul has been freed; it is mature, advancing barefoot in blood and muck. Doesn't God always advance this way on Earth? Only the faint-hearted can despair over the ruin of the flesh. Perhaps the tilling of the flesh, as with the fields, is necessary for the new seed. May God grant the Greek field a like fate! This wretched race, our race, is unsettled. But we ten or more souls exist. My hope is indomitable, my determination increases to undertake a risky campaign against degeneration and wretchedness, and to create from this Greek clay the model of Divinity. God is never molded from success, glory and comfort. Only from shame, dishonor and tears. Greece is a lost cause. Let's undertake it. Only the ambitious and merchants love sure situations. When I think about you working for the children of the future, when I feel my heart burning with pride because I work without hope of reward, you can't imagine how strongly I feel united with you in the fiery air of effort. And my joy is great when I feel you beside me. Is that not a great reward?

* * *

Cherie, I just now got your letter. My God, I'm so much in agreement with you over the wretchedness of the Greek and I would really like you to agree with me that "so much the better!" I have a deep conviction that all this wretchedness is needed in order for salvation to come. More on that later. We won't die, Comrade, before our turn. It's coming, it's coming, it's coming! You don't know what faith I have and what hidden indomitable determination. The whole world is reeling, struggling, collapsing; this can't go on for long. We must get ready, and all the preparations are being made. They degenerate, dishonor and become brutalized; we learn to become disgusted and to hate and to be inflexible. Do you remember the dream I had of you where with tightly drawn lips you said: "Yes! Yes!"? It is for me a shining, unmistakable herald of the future. I'm certain that your soul will then be wonderfully brave; and I feel that I won't degenerate. Write me like that, tell me everything, denounce people and events. I want to see everything happening down there through your eyes. And here I am working, following the Bolshevik movement, getting prepared. Let the God of vengeance hear our cry soon.

Concerning the two financial matters you wrote me about:

1) Sperandzas: As you know we owe Farandatos 9,000 drachmas from the Prastova affair. To pay off the debt I signed a contract with him (notarized by Synodinos) authorizing him to collect the money from Sperandzas for the Greek texts I wrote. Anyway, the first 9,000 belong to Farandatos and he together with Fotakis undertook the blackmailing of Sperandzas.

2) We needn't feel any concern over our shares. It doesn't matter to us how much they go up or down. The income always remains the same; one English pound each. No cause for uneasiness.

Nevertheless! Look how just yesterday, Sunday, when I was feeling very depressed here in my room, I said to myself that we are just butchers, cowards and hypocrites. There is only one courageous act: To throw aside whatever you have, fortune, comfort, habit and to go into the streets and shout! How are the great distinguished from the mediocre? Only thus. "Abandon all" as Plotinus commanded. Divest yourself of everything as Saint Francis did. Ownership is the source of every misery. When will I be able to do it? You were always more courageous, I remember, in financial matters. But sometimes here of late my heart has been shaken with disgust and has shouted at me. Who knows, my soul is so ripe (so beyond every earthly desire) that sometimes I feel horrified when I think that the great moment of my deliverance may be nearing.

Cherie, my beloved wife, Comrade, if I could only do one deed that would seem worthy of you!

N.

∽∾∾∾

LETTER 44

Cherie, I just received your letter and the newspapers. The six scapegoats of Greece have by now been put to death, so the grief in your letter has no meaning any longer. They should have been killed by the people but it is fortunate at least that Plastiras was there and spoke courageously. It is better for us to perish acting in a tragedy than to live playing an operetta. Here all Europe is beside itself with this barbarity! But it remained totally impassive over the 50,000 that lost their homes and over all those thousands of Turks that were killed by the Greeks. For my part I was glad, because I think that only now will the Greeks understand that something important is happening. They don't care if Smyrna, Constantinople and Thrace are lost. But, for their shepherds to have been killed like dogs, the very ones that frequented Dore[1], will fill them with amazement and dread. And dread is always useful to such a nation.

Here, I'm going through a slow but sure development. I don't know, but for the first time in my life I'm interested in my race in the same way that I'm interested in all races. Of course, if I examine myself more deeply, the representatives of the human race that are closest to my heart today are the Russians. I feel that they are today's bearers of divinity. I'm learning Russian now and I'll try to go to Russia and to prepare for your coming as well. We have to live as long as we can in that divine, that horrible, that magnificent chaos of Russia. The books I'm reading concerning the present-day situation in some of the provinces of Russia speak of horrifying things — of hunger, misery and violence. And yet at the same time of an unimaginable exaltation. Until now, it has always been· one person who has tried to save the human race, the founder of a religion. Now a whole nation has undertaken this deadly mission. The suffering of one is now multiplied by millions; pain wracks countless souls. I have no illusions about contemporary reality in Russia. I know that its own leaders have no clear idea of their mission and I know that the people suffer unimaginably. I have met the greatest Russian philosopher of today, Schestov², and a writer, Remizov, both of·whom left Russia because they were opposed to the regime and were unable to tolerate the terrible details. I also know that an idea remains pure and untainted, without blood and muck, only in the heated head of an idealist. But at the same time it is completely barren, sterile and superfluous. As soon as an idea appears on this earth of ours, it's fouled, bloodied and misused by thousands of men — but that's how it becomes a mother, enriches life and lifts the spirit of the struggling God a bit higher. I'm disgusted with these romantic conceptions of the Idea. The Idea is like God — through unimaginable crimes, dishonesty and stupidity it nevertheless advances slowly, with toil, clambering up the rugged earth. Our duty is to try and find the rhythm of God's course and then to adjust the rhythm of our small, ephemeral life to it, as well as we can. Only then can we mortals succeed in achieving something immortal because then we will be working together with something Eternal. Thus also may our life — our action and our thought — acquire unity and character. We overcome petty detail, we overcome boredom, we overcome the narrowness of the heart, we feel that men and all peoples and what's more, all plants and all animals are working together and that we all ascend together, swept up by a mysterious and invisible Life-Force. Where are we going? No one knows. Don't ask, ascend! Perhaps we are going nowhere, perhaps there is no reward for the daily grind of life. So much the better! For thus we overcome the last and greatest temptation — Hope. We fight because we want to, without rewards; we are not mercenaries. We sing even though we know there is no one to listen to us, we work though there is no master to pay us a day's wages at nightfall. We are without hope, serene and free. This is true heroism, the highest feat, it seems to me, of man.

Ah, my beloved wife, I can't tell you how sweetly and peacefully I'm living these days in this vision of hopelessness. I'm working on *Buddha*, I'm preparing to go to Russia; who knows, maybe I'll be able to attune my worthless life to a worthy cause. After *Buddha* I no longer want to write art, I want to go through the Russian experience and then try to find a way to formulate the religious vision which possesses me. We'll see.

* * *

Always
N.

LETTER 45

22-11-22

Cherie, I just received your letter where you tell me that it is not worth sacrificing oneself for the contemporary Greek and that I have the right to stay away, selfishly working for myself.

In your first letter, where you said exactly the opposite, I replied that one thing is certain: We should never make our actions dependent on the worth of the masses. Our duty is to act; all the rest, reward and recognition, do not concern us. To cry, to cry in the wilderness! This seems to me our simplest and most fruitful duty.

We have to do only one thing before acting: To see if we, the doers, are ready. To see if our entire soul and flesh is pressed by the need, physical and "inner", to go into the wilderness and cry out. Because if we go there immature, following only our logic or the example of others, enraged with the cowardice of others, then we destroy ourselves and are of benefit to no one.

I wrote to you that 1) I don't feel I am ready. I haven't managed to overcome Art yet, much less the Absurd.

2) When I've overcome these two, the human material I use will not be Greek.

I have decided to go to Russia. I don't know when. I must get ready. Now I'm learning Russian and one of these days I'll go to a craftsman near here and learn a trade — carpentry. In that way I'll be able to work in Russia for three hours a day and I'll go round the villages. There I'll test the Word that I bring.

I'm trying hard to be calm, to keep my mind serene above the chaos of madness. I want to finish some of the writings I've started as well as *Buddha*. I'll send them to you to have them printed and thus be relieved. Then I'll abandon this paper and ink and perhaps I'll try hunger and horror, those terrible primordial Mothers. I'm ashamed that my life is so bourgeois, so prudent, that my room is warm and my clothes correct. I am ashamed that at this terrible hour when the soul of the world is collapsing, I am holding a pen and putting words together. I read this the other day in a Russian story: "After the year 2000, wise men, politicians and other leaders of free states were having a banquet at the

North Pole. They ate and drank a lot and then started to make toasts. A woman got up and said, 'In a city at the South Pole people are starving. I am ashamed to sit with the well-fed, I will go to that city down there with the starved. There is where I belong!' "

I feel that that woman is my soul.

Lefteris talked with the intellectuals of Athens and their response was cold, unsympathetic and ironical. Greece has not yet an ear to listen with. I talked to some Russians and Poles I met here about the face of the struggling God and from that moment their life changed. They tell me that now they know why they fight, why they seek freedom, why their heart is one with the mass of the oppressed while in the past their struggles were feeble because they were following the arguments of a narrow, anemic logic.

Russia! Hungry masses, tilled and ready souls. What you say about Greece is absolutely right and living here I've thought about it many times. A violent revolution from "above" benefits no one. People follow in bewilderment for a moment but soon go back like a bear, with a sigh of relief to their former misery, and are always worse off. We must first, with patience and perseverance, work with the masses for long years, to enlighten them, to awaken in them the sleeping God and then . . . and then what? Then, by itself, from "below", from the roots, the overthrow will come and all the flowers of evil will drop off.

In Greece we need such an enlightenment. Books, newspapers, lectures, schools, a vanguard that will perish, great adversity, preparation of the soil. When I analyze my capabilities I feel that I do not have enough patience for so much preparation. In me the need is compelling, it cannot wait. It seems to me that the sense of harmony I'm living with is so simple that as soon as it's spelled out it will enlighten and toughen the soul. Sometimes, in the evening, at the terrible moment when the lamps are lit, I feel desperate and my heart seizes up. But then again I take courage, I look upon myself, upon humans, animals and ideas with mercy. Ah! if we could only perish suddenly by serving a Purpose. Which Purpose? Does this earth, this starlight have a purpose? What do we care? Don't ask, fight! Let us define a Purpose ourselves, let us regulate our lives according to the Purpose we set. Then our acts, our words and our moods will acquire a unity and will harmonize with this Purpose. And we must consider this harmonization as our duty, that is, our happiness.

I received the newspapers and I thank you very much. All the wretchedness of the Greek is there. Indemnities and slander. Those that kept silent or cheered during the previous regime now come out as defenders of the revolution. We are ignorant, cowardly and petty. I would be terrified by the idea that we belong to such a race if I didn't know that honest souls are fortified by exactly such a climate and don't run any risk (because of obstinacy, pride and disgust) of degenerating. Here, I try as hard as I can to work, deriving my courage from the horror that our infamous countrymen produce in me. Do likewise yourself. Let's keep all our strength because we may need it all to spend on a positive and no longer negative action.

* * *

N.

ᘒᘒᘒ

LETTER 47

Cherie, I'll immediately reply to everything you wrote. 1) I won't become a worker only out of romanticism or utopianism. I have never been a vapid idealist, nor have I been that enthusiastic about the working masses. It's just that at the moment if you want to stay in Russia, you have to work three hours a day. I must declare what work I do in order to get past the border. If I say writer and the like it will be difficult for them to let me in and I'll be under observation. I must find a trade. That is why I am going to learn a craft. I'm awaiting some information from an acquaintance of a friend of mine in Russia to tell me which craft is most needed there so I'll have a better chance of staying.

I'm learning Russian so that I won't be completely alien to the Russian way of life. I have no illusions — unfortunately. If I had illusions I would overcome the absurd, I would make the efforts you advise me to make and become a man of action.

Up to now my strength has been thinking and writing. The first I manage all right and I'm not ashamed to admit it. I feel my brain is solid, of very good quality, very bright. The second, the writing, I manage only fairly well. My art is not clear, pure, great. The colors choke the spirituality of the line, there are too many images and they are expressed with exaggeration. I haven't managed to find simplicity, to overcome the showy and ornamental. My heart (I say it even if you don't believe it) suffers deeply. Maybe you don't believe it because its suffering isn't over petty details concerning myself or another definite person; maybe for this reason it appears impassive and selfish. However, I don't know if many people on this earth today ache and suffer as much as I do. If I'm away from you, if I'm far away from my country, if I wander everywhere without finding peace anywhere, if I now want to go to Russia, all this arises not from extreme joy but from extreme pain. I have agonies greater than my personal vicissitudes and I have needs that I know I'll never be able to fulfill. Nothing can give me even the slighest joy. I stay in this room all day, I read and write and I feel such disgust for these petty occupations that often

I cannot stop myself from weeping. I often listen to music, attend lectures, watch dance performances, go to museums — and all these are like the apples of Dante, they fill my mouth with ashes.

You tell me to come down to Greece and preach the return of the Greeks to Asia Minor.[1] This doesn't correspond to any inner need of mine. I know that civilization has always been born from within these horrid, deadly uprootings. If our aim is *to transubstantiate matter into spirit* then this misfortune of the Greeks will later, after many generations, lead to one of two results: Either to the destruction of this Hellenism or to ascension, a new blooming within the blood and tears of a Cry. Both are good. To break comfortable habits, to renounce happiness, is indispensible; it is a prerequisite, I would say, for all ascension.

You'll tell me that I am far away and apathetically contemplate these creatures that perish and that I don't see the infamy, the hunger and the streets full of these human wrecks. Yes, I'm far away and that's why I see with more clarity and with greater perspective. If we let ourselves be carried away with these everyday details, these completely bloody images, then it will be impossible for us to place this great adventure of the Greek race in a perspective of time larger than our own small lives. I can see all these human waves beyond my times, beyond the cry of my heart, and I know that through such violent flux and mixings of Europe and Asia, Greece has always managed to shoot forth the flower of art and mind.

I write and write to you; my heart is suffocating, I know that you will respond to these words as though they were the abstract theories of a mind which, without feeling, sets up humans and nations like pawns in an imaginary chess game. I have no greater grief and I'm still not used to it. In all the world I want only you to believe in me and accept my words as they come out of my breast. And it is precisely you who have never believed in the sincerity of my suffering. I'm struggling to draw forth strength from within the tragic part of my fate.

Thus I'm trying hard to be able to enjoy the terrible wilderness of my life and to ripen my thought on such a hopeless road. I don't always succeed. I often look upon the hope of death with relief. No doubt the most positive good that I have got from your lack of confidence in me is not to care, not to be frightened by death. What do I have to lose?

* * *

⟋ᴖᴗᴖ⟍

LETTER 48

Cherie, I just this minute received your letter. Nothing grieves me more deeply than when you write that I have forgotten you. I think my only hope in this terrible life is to know that you understand me and that I remember you and that I love you as nothing else in the world. Last night when I went to bed I was so sad that I couldn't keep the tears back. All this struggle for what? For what do I sacrifice all the joy I would have being with you? What does all the phantasmagoria of life rend our small, ephemeral heart of flesh in such a complex, incurable and invincible way? My life here is bound in struggles; I write, read, listen to music and nothing can console me. I'm working on a plan to go to Russia and I know what awaits me there as well, so I cannot entirely give myself up to the joy and illusions of the new trip. Sometimes the *Buddha* that I'm writing now gives me some consolation. I've also started a new book, *The Saviors of God.*[1] But when I put my pen down, I am desolate, I am not contained in all these alphabetical symbols I arrange in lines. When a letter of yours is good, I feel a great joy, as also I do when I get a letter from Lefteris. I don't know; the idea that a small legion is being formed, that a few of us believe in a Utopią enchants me so much that my reason becomes dumbstruck and I feel completely fitted to a metaphysical, fervent endeavor. Must I concentrate all my struggle within this fiery and vain circle? Must I force myself to believe that this circle is not vain, not a new invention of my fertile mind? I'm writing *The Saviors of God* now, a mystical book in which I trace the method whereby the soul ascends from cycle to cycle until it reaches the supreme Contract. There are five cycles: Ego, Humanity, Earth, Universe, God. I describe how to climb all these steps and how we are able to live simultaneously all the previous cycles after we reach the supreme point. I'm deliberately writing it without poetry, in a dry, imperative form. I'm telling you a lot about it because it is the latest fruit of my search. When will the search end? Or is it that my purpose is only the search itself, that is, the progression from point to point? Does God himself perhaps progress in that way? Perhaps this search (upward and with coherence) is the purpose of the Universe. Purpose and means become identified.

Only the weak set a Goal and feel appeased when they reach it. The tireless, when they reach it, then transfer it. God is the supreme expression of this tireless and struggling element. He is the indestructible and incurable Seeker.

Our duty is to identify our ephemeral way with his. To seek, indestructibly and incurably. He who succeeds at this continues doing it after a certain age (30 or 40), he who doesn't restrict the Divine Flow in himself, is inconsolably happy and at the same time a faithful reflection of God who is equally unhappy and heroic. Which road shall we take? The human voice, the flesh, laziness, habit and conformity, constantly urge us to stop, to go round and round, always round the same point. No matter how lofty this point is, it's a sin to stay eternally at it. But at the same time it insures human success; you rejoice, you make others rejoice and you leave solid work behind, a sure and holy example.

Cherie, I cannot tell you how clearly, without lyricism, without illusion and exultation, I see the pattern my steps trace on this earth. The way I make out my course is so clear that it's like a geometric theorem. I don't feel ashamed telling you all this over and over because even you sometimes think my head is full of fantasies and that I want, for example, to become a worker in Russia from just pure romanticism. No so-called practical person has a more stable and clearer mind than mine. The difference is, however, that the circle my sight embraces is infinitely larger and consequently it seems utopian.

* * *

N.

∽∽∽

LETTER 49

Cherie, I'll answer your letter immediately. No one is more disgusted than me with the cynical observer (because I was one formerly). When I say we must not set the homeland as the goal of our action, I am not saying we should cross our arms and look down from above ("from above" here meaning unfeeling and impotent) onto the spectacle of the people, but rather that we shift our activity to a more vigorous and wider plane in the broader circle of the struggle — that is, to Man, without the label of Greek or Turk, to the wretched and miraculous thing that walks the earth and loves and suffers. At first, men cared only for themselves, later for their families and their homes, after that for their race and homeland and at last for Man. There have always been men throughout the ages, from Prometheus to Lenin, who have fought for Man. But the struggle was chaotic, satanic, it didn't incite the masses. Now we must fight to form this new armed camp, to teach people (first setting the example ourselves) to breathe outside boundaries, to suffer and be glad when the people in China and Russia suffer or are glad.

It requires an ever harsher, crueler struggle because first we must conquer sentimental conceptions within ourselves. It requires intense daily effort, for our heart has not yet become accustomed to the new cycle and still easily falls into the old habits or stops altogether in unfeeling observation. It requires great clarity of mind to know what each nation should contribute to the common struggle and how each race must be molded and armed (politically, educationally, intellectually, artistically, religiously. . .) in order to be of use, to take its place like a piece in a mosaic in the picture of the created God.

From this last need — clarity of mind — we understand what great work every thinker must do for his own race. Trying to find exactly what separates it from other races and what to cultivate in order that it will be more useful in the pan-human assault. By doing thus he will know what he is working for. He will know that his race is a means and not an end, and this he will now know for certain for he will have been saved from the restrictive iron collar of his homeland; because of this his activity and his influence in school, in society and so forth, will be of a completely different quality than before.

What will the activity be then of a Greek intellectual concerning his race? Since we're examining the problem generally we'll formulate the question in the same way. The answer depends on the development of each person. Is it necessary to outline a common stance from this very moment? I think it is better to leave the thinkers for a while to try out their solutions. I, for example, think that the virtues of our race can come to fire only outside the establishment. As a citizen of a State, the Greek is awful, but as Odysseus, wandering, working, trading, thinking, without his own system of government (as the Jews), he is unique in the world. He could, as the Jews, become extremely active yeast for the rising of the earth.

This opinion of mine appears criminal. It is very premature and would be very dangerous if it were to be put into effect now that nationalistic conscience is hardening and narrowing the people. The personality of the Greek race might be endangered if it were violently assimilated by nationalist peoples.

If I were a politician, I would not only not have mentioned this idea but I wouldn't have even had it. But since I only think, I have the right to see and to desire that which is far beyond present need.

Ah! how difficult it is to speak in letters. For one is not able to guess what objections there may be and to pause until the objection is settled. Your idea can be perfectly combined with this conception I'm writing to you about. Whoever feels the need of the race overflowing in him can work perfectly well having only the race as his goal and working only within that circle. But this same person or the broader thinker (that is, the one who works in a broader circle that contains the above as well) must know that the race is a medium for working in a larger homeland, the Earth. And this comprehension will regulate his hate, his love and his contribution.

* * *

Always yours
N.

LETTER 51

20-1-23

* * *

Here I am working again, in despair. I wake up at dawn and now that the room isn't heated I stay in bed and work. I'm writing *The Saviors of God* as I mentioned to you. I don't know if you will like it. It is written tersely, a laborious climb from circle to circle. I don't know, all of these are like commands out of a past time which I'm executing now at this moment though I have proceeded further on. If only I could make the "leap". To leave writing and poetry behind me on the other shore and speak to men without judging, without shyness and without weighing every word. It seems that only then will I find the form wherein my spirit can breathe comfortably. To be able to speak to men, not to one or two, but to masses of men. To intermix my ideas with contemporary needs — economical, sociological and political. To speak and move men concerning the contemporary problems of their everyday life. The idea (abstract, fleshless, philosophical) can't satisfy the carnivorous soul. And everything is clear and whole in my mind but I lack the strength to leap over the fence and defeat the Absurd. Will I never be able to? If not, my life will be the deepest, most incurable bitterness and trial. And so what you said to Skipis[1] is in truth my only worth — I struggle, I look ahead like Odysseus, but without knowing if I will ever anchor in Ithaca. Unless Ithaca is the voyage itself.

* * *

Always yours

N.

LETTER 54

* * *

Yesterday the Kastanakis's and I went to an exhibition of contemporary Indian art. They wanted me to take them and somehow initiate them into that art. We kept talking about you. Here we have an inflamed, exquisite soul; not too many exist like it in the world. If only she lived in different surroundings! A while ago I saw a woman addressing a communist demonstration here. How envious I felt. Her voice clear, decisive, penetrating amidst the vague opinions of men. She said without theories and references to Marx that "words are superfluous" and that "the moment of action has arrived. Are we right, are we wrong? Only through action will we see. This world has to be destroyed!" Another woman, 70 years old, Clara Zetkin, sneaked across the frontier and appears at every single communist demonstration all over Germany and speaks with passion, impetus and incredible clarity. Thousands of workers march through the large boulevards with this old woman. Another woman, ugly and lame, is the director of a famous school for proletarians on the outskirts of Berlin. The other day they had a conference and all the "Committed Reformers" went and talked, not any longer about *new pedagogical methods* but about the *new aims* that pedagogics must be given. Whenever Tanni, the lame director, passed by, there were whistles, curses and stones from the children of the bourgeois schools. Everybody hates her in that suburb, Spandau. Only her pupils, boys and girls 10-14 years old, adore her. There are battles among the children and the lame Tyrtaias ignites hatred, tenderness and love for the coming war.

I always think of you when I look at these women. Should you start in Greece? Maybe your small light will fade out but that way one helps the future hero. I don't know what our duty is. For myself, if I were stronger, I would stay in Greece, I would fight and perish. Now I struggle to be saved, living in a more fertile soil, and maybe I'll become so strong that I will perish quietly, fighting, fighting those wretched Greeks.

* * *

About Kondoglou![1] A peasant, a classsic ingrate. But it doesn't matter, if he still writes beautifully. Don't talk to him, just notice with pity and fear, what muck the spirit sometimes chooses to live in. Ah! human beings, those exquisite and dreadful organisms, how they pollute the face of God. But it seems that God is less demanding than we are. Or maybe he is stronger and is able to put up with the ugliness. Last night I dreamed continually of Jenny. Is there anything wrong with her? Write me, love me, don't forget me.

N.

LETTER 60

Cherie, I think it is a long time since I've had a letter from you and I'm worried. My heart is full of anxieties, worry and agitation. I finished *The Saviors of God* yesterday. Is it good? I don't know. I tried with simple words, as a confession, to trace the spiritual struggles of my life, where I began, how I overcame obstacles, how God's struggle began, and how I found the central meaning that now regulates my thought, reason and action. Oh! they are not completely regulated yet, a multitude of bad habits from my previous development still prevent me from moving in accordance with the strict inflexible command of God. But I'm struggling, consciously now, to remain faithful to the essence of my life.

I find myself in a new no-man's land. The ultimate, the most sacred form of theory, is action. God is everywhere, in man, in politics, in everyday life, and he's in danger. He isn't omnipotent and he can't simply cross his arms and await his certain victory. His salvation depends on us. And only if he is saved, may we be saved. Theory has value only as a preparation; the critical struggle lies in the act.

I live this new need every minute. A Purpose must be found for which all of us can work, to which we can devote ourselves, to be saved or to perish with it. Only thus can we overcome the tediousness of life, the wretchedness of men and objects and put forth our maximum force. The Purpose must be deeply united (without being completely absorbed) in the contemporary social and political struggle. This world must be destroyed, it must exist no more! The first duty this Purpose must undertake is hate. The second duty is to find the nucleus of the coming civilization. To transubstantiate hate into something higher, that is, into a means and not into an end. The aim of hate is Love. What will be the shape of this new Love? For without a basis in Love the elevation of man can have no meaning. But Love changes in every civilization and this change is the new element that the great Revolutionaries seek everywhere, though they do not always find it.

Yesterday, I was at a conference of the "Progressives." It is a wonderful, aggressive group of men, mainly child educators, who call for the complete reformation of the School. Not to change the method but to change the goal of child education. They are all communists and extreme socialists. I'll write you another time about the three excellent men who lead the struggle. They have conferences, speak in all the cities, are poor, wear *peau de diable* and dark, open-necked proletarian shirts. They publish magazines, books and manifestos. I'm a member of this conference and one of the most extreme. At the conference the other day a young teacher talked about the School of

Wyneken (Wyneken is one of the most advanced thinkers and child educators in the world today. He founded an excellent school with a new pedagogical system, in the woods. He was charged with being a homosexual and put in prison. He is still there). The speaker extolled the splendid school — the forest, the music, the freedom, the fervent love of the body and of the mind, the passion for beauty.

I couldn't take it. I shouted, I interrupted, I didn't like it at all. When the discussion began I said that the School of today shouldn't be a refuge, an island of beauty in an ocean of modern ugliness. It shouldn't deal with art and ideals or be a sacred retreat. Today the School should have one and only one aim — Preparation. Preparation for the immediate, contemporary, already begun struggle. It shouldn't be an idyll, far away in a forest. The School today should be in everyday surroundings (later, when we win, we can worry about beauty), the ugly places where the growing student will live and work in the future. These ugly surroundings must be well-examined by teacher and students so they can come to hate them and try to change them. They must avoid making it ideal because such vain hope ends with people losing heart. They must change the ugly surroundings as much as they can. By all means, let them make an excursion to the forest, let them desire the sea and the air but let them know that today there is not enough time. And further I would say that it is not necessary (as in the school of Wyneken) that all be just, regular and perfect. The students must learn when they are being wronged and to resist this injustice and cry out. Not just to eat regularly everyday but often to be hungry and thirsty and to suffer. To have strong bodies not for beauty's sake but to be strong. What will they use their strength for? To learn early that everything they are taught, all the strength they are gathering, the education, the endurance, the longing, has one and only one aim — the destruction of the old (the world of their parents) and the creation of the new.

These days the aims of the School must be clear, implacable and narrow. Later, when we win, with the might of our God, then we'll see. Then there will be time for art, music and the idyllic life. And if we are still alive, we, the vanguard, will again put down mines for new destruction and creation. But our life is short. We must work within the time we have while we are alive. We must understand our historical moment and the vanguard of that moment and straight away, decisively and without compromise, place ourselves at the foremost bastion in the battle. We must not recognize any other duty, virtue or happiness.

My God, Cherie, may I be able, may I only be able to overcome the last remnants of my old human form and to throw myself, not only with my thought, but with my voice, with my body, onto that foremost bastion of my God! I know that today only the smallest number of men have seen Duty with such clarity and passion. And I fight to make the last leap to the other shore leaving shame and cowardice behind me. Ah! if only I were Russian! If only I were able to speak to the Russians! Today there is no other soul so ready!

I'm pining away. Oh! if only you knew how I suffer, without hope, yet without any lack of courage. The joys I had before are no more. Music must be exceptional to dominate me for a moment. But I resist, I don't want this opium of beauty. I feel (as Dhemel said, remember) "Wife, my child, we have no time."[1] Sometimes a new painting carries me away, not because it's beautiful but because it is a cry of protest, a color, a line which is raised within a small wooden frame and is protesting. Now that I have seen Sent Mahesa[2] dance I no longer want to see dancing. I saw the highest there is. The dance no longer interests me. Sent Mahesa danced only once and left for her villa in Munich. I no longer go to the old museums. They are revered, static forms of other periods. Today a living heart finds them not only strange but odious. Often these forms of beauty lead the most select souls astray and take them from our painful, ugly and uncertain contemporary duty.

I'm getting further away from many of my friends — I wrote to Sikelianos that our roads have split and that we can no longer go on together. His life seems phony and outdated to me. May God grant him great poems and may he not become completely lost. Sfakianakis no longer exists for me. I love and respect him but what does he stand for? What does he contribute to the struggle? That's all I want to know.

You alone contribute, you are vigilant, you fight, you worry, hate and protest amid the cowardly Greek crowd. It is my destiny, however, not to live with you. I have no greater grief. Because I know there is no cure for my destiny even if I return.

At least, write me. Don't forget that I exist. Don't forget that I exist and love you.

N.

LETTER 62

10-4-23

Cherie, I am now collecting all the communist schoolbooks and children's books that have been written and I am beginning to execute my old plan of writing a series of books for the children of the coming society. We must be ready. Later I will write Histories based on the social struggle showing how one class predominates, now the king, now the nobility, the clergy, the bourgeoisie; showing how civilizations are created and abolished; showing how we must now set conscientiously the foundations of a new victory and a new civilization.

I'm thinking of founding a polemical group of different nationalities here and one of its aims will be to write such children's books, each in terms of his own nation but with the same general polemical and creative direction.

A little while ago I returned from seeing a famous Russian-Jewish poet who translated Homer, etc. into Hebraic verse. We spoke for two hours. My God, when I come into contact with these famous contributors to the contemporary spiritual struggle my confidence and faith in myself grow beyond description. All those I have met I consider to be my inferiors. I speak with them up to a point but beyond that we are unable to proceed. These last months my mind has acquired a sure decisive direction. The secret fertile theories that gladdened my soul up until now have enabled me to see my epoch and my duty with great clarity.

Destruction, destruction, destruction! All the present-day infamy and wretchedness must collapse. Each in his own area must destroy, preach hate and prepare the generations. If I were dropped off in any part of the world my first work would be to found a school. To ready the combatants, to teach them, in accordance with the flame which consumes me, the history of Greece, Rome and modern times. To teach them why they must become good workers, good teachers, good scientists, good and fertile fathers. To teach them how to read a poem, how to observe the stars, the animals, men and ideas. Single-mindedness, conscious, implacable and irreconcilable single-mindedness. Not useless theories, general views that say this is good, that is good, the opposite is good, all is good or all is bad. No the world is divided into two; good and evil, up and down, God and Anti-God. What does it mean that we are soldiers of God? It means that our duty is to hate one half of the world's direction and to love the other. Later when an equilibrium has been achieved (later, that is, after our victory) let them teach men to live in harmony, to be universal and tolerant. At the moment such virtues are weaknesses and an abandonment of the shield of our fight.

Suddenly, while I happened to be talking to two or three men yesterday, I felt myself become so angry and violent that I stopped and was glad that I was ruled by so much faith. I write you this as a portent of deep change in me. It is the portent of action. Perhaps some time must pass yet; I must liberate myself from the remnants of past fascinations, I must be delivered of *Buddha* which I'm writing now, I must be rid of poetry. This must happen "internally", as fruit ripens. There are several places I must see to be rescued from their temptation. I must pass through it all with my own personal idiosyncratic system, that is, slowly and exhaustively. Only in this way can I proceed without looking behind me. When I argue with anyone now and he attempts to refute me, I hasten to list all his arguments and find others he doesn't know about. And why? Because I have lived in his situation for years and I know all of its secrets, "I've been in the know." I've been against the spoken language, then for it, nationalist, scientist, poet, socialist, religious fanatic, atheist, aesthete — and none of these can seduce me any longer.

* * *

Write me, always yours

N.

LETTER 63

Cherie, I would very much like us to talk together about

everything you wrote in order to reach a conclusion concerning the Myrsines and the Papandreous.[1] The results of whatever I would say to you would be more or less the following:

We must be irreconcilable in our ideas for two reasons:

1) So that the small number of our pure and brave don't lose their way. We must be the light that burns at the end of the road and that shows the way.

2) To compel, by derision and goading, to incite men of action to be as demanding of themselves as the inflexibility of reality allows and never to be satisfied.

We must clearly separate the nature of the Idea from the need of Action. The nature of the Idea is to want the Absolute, to be disgusted with compromise and not to accept any retreat. Woe to the Idea which would capitulate and be happy in relativity.

The nature of action is adaptive. Enormous and all powerful is the inflexibility of habit, the insistence on the past, the wretchedness of human nature that doesn't want to go regularly through the terrible, laborious resurrection of creative renovation.

What happens if a man, a standard-bearer of an Idea, manages to come to authority and to give a new rhythm to the enormous sluggish bulk of society? One of two things: 1) Not wanting to yield, to accept compromises, he turns with disdain from action and once more takes refuge in the lofty region of his idea. 2) He fights for years, he sacrifices one thing to be successful in ten, he makes detours to impose his idea without a deadly collision. When he succeeds, we say (generations or centuries later), "Here we have the highest sort of idealist, who, rather than yield, forced life to take on his rhythm." And only he knows what concessions he made, what he wanted and what he managed to get, and he looks at his work with horror, because he sees the miserable, criminal, often idiotic caricature of his attempt.

Here I'm copying for you some words of Lenin from one
of his statements at the conference in Moscow in November,
1921.

"Il faut revenir en arrière, battre en retraite. Les
concessions que nous avons faites sont insuffisantes. .
. . Reconnaissons nos fautes. Nous en sommes
arrivés à un recul non seulement dans le capitalisme
mais ver la réglémentation de commerce, vers la
reconnaissance de l'argent. Il faut donc regarder le
péril en face et ne pas cacher à la classe ouvrière
notre march en arrière."[2]

One of the biggest, bloodiest dramas a man čan follow
is the life of Lenin. Here I can follow close at hand all the
convulsions of his bitterness, his struggle and his implacable
attempt. He fights, yields, attacks, accepts the opposite of
what he believes; he feels his idea being degraded by reality,
he publishes laws and recognizes commerce, ownership,
money, private enterprise; he attempts to transfuse into the
gigantic body of Russia as much new blood as it is able to
accept. In the fullness of time after some generations all
these compromises will have been organized into one new
creation. The entire work will be presented, great and
without details; all the bloody tragedy of Lenin, the day to
day one, will be confined to two or three incidents because
the work itself will answer all questions. (The same thing
happened with Christ, Buddha, every reformer.)

Why am I writing you all this? All this has no relation to
those nobodies who behave indecently all the time in
Greece. All of them make compromises not for the sake of
an Idea but for the sake of their little selves, so they can get
to the top. All of them, being clever Greeks, in order to get
themselves a good position use as their instrument and
weapon whatever men find sacred.

But I am writing you about this because we must reach
a general agreement on the subject. It is possible that

sometime you will come to a responsible position; you will
then feel fantastic bitterness and either resign immediately
or, in order to realize as much of your idea as it is now
possible for the Greek reality to accept, make concessions,
crying, cursing, hating (yourself and others). If you ever
become the director of a prison, do not forget my words of
today. I've passed through this hell. No one is as ready as I
am, at any moment, to throw away the position that was
given to him. But I stayed for a year, struggling, dying every
day, to save some people in the Pontos,[3] to see that the
children in the orphanages of Macedonia had somewhat
better fare, to see that some families were somewhat better
established in Thrace. What did I expect? Countless things.
What did I manage to do in that position? Nearly nothing.
The tiniest amount, for which I paid dearly.

* * *

Lately, I've been planning to start a new book —
completely revolutionary and exclusively for Greece. The
argument I wrote concerning Wyneken's school continues to
irritate me. A little while ago I made a general outline of the
book. I'll speak of the content the modern Greek school
must have. I'll speak about our time, about Greek reality
and what it is, and how we must rear and prepare the new
generation. A completely communistic book without any
compromise, a revolutionary manifesto with the school
problems as its motive.

* * *

N.

LETTER 64

May 1

Cherie, I've just come back from a large gathering of communists at a big square in Berlin. It was in front of the Palace, thousands of people had gathered, the square was full of red flags, the statues of the old Hohenzollerns were all decorated in red flags, with hammers and sickles. Mothers had their small children on their shoulders so that they could see and have the spectacle imprinted on their minds. Many orators, well-known phrases; the mob listened for two or three hours to the eternal phraseology and dispersed.

I had with me an intellectual German communist, dressed in the way communist intellectuals dress here (students, teachers, writers, etc.) — full buttoned coats, *peau de diable*, opened collars, usually colored, no hats, short pants, socks up to the knees and thick-soled shoes or sandals. I was telling him how this form of mass meeting seemed out-dated and soulless to me. We have to find a new form for these gatherings and for communist organizations. These mass meetings are for today what religious processions were in the past. How did the Church organize these processions? In the streets an entire dramatic event unfolded. There were choruses, one would speak, the other would answer, the bishop making a visual unity; they would stop at a crossroad, they would entreat God, and the crowd would grow silent, suddenly to burst forth in invocations, threats and hopes.

It wouldn't be the same, but these processions could give us some ideas. We must organize in modern forms the enthusiasm, the hate and the power of the proletariat when it pours into the streets for mass meetings or protests.

And the form must be different for each nation. How did the Germans do it in the Middle Ages when they were starting off on Crusades or when they were struggling for generations to throw off feudalism? In this way we'll be led to a modern form of a mass meeting that is purely Germanic.

My friend agreed with me but said that either we lack the great individuals able to grasp the subconscious desires of the crowd or these subconscious desires are not powerful enough yet to impose themselves on certain individuals and be given concrete forms.

I regularly work together with this friend and some others to found an international league for the enlightenment of the people through books, lectures, propaganda, etc. The others mainly insist on the training of select individuals who will deal with the philosophical, scientific and artistic subjects, from the Communist-Marxist point of view. I insist on the urgency of leaving all these intellectual luxuries for the moment and seeing how we will address ourselves to 1) people in general, 2) the workers in particular, 3) the children.

Sometime, I'll write you more about it.

* * *

N.

◆◆◆

LETTER 66

Cherie, I just received your letter. All the things Danilidis says seem to me like missionary weak tea, well-known European recipes for coming to grips with reality ("Greek reality" as the fashionable phrase goes) and acting accordingly. What wretchedness, what poverty, what cowardice! Greek reality cries in us; the only sure way to find it is to listen to our Greek heart, which better than any campaign of documents, knows what it wants. What can our people tell us that we don't know better than they? If it is true that we represent not our small ego but a whole Greek people and what is more a whole contemporary people who fight within contemporary needs and seek freedom, then our duty is one — to state in word or deed this cry of our heart. And it is only then that the people will clearly feel (for the first time) how they suffer and why they suffer and which is the way to deliverance. Today the people suffer and attribute their bad fate now to politics, now to poverty and now to ignorance. But when we speak they will learn that their suffering is much deeper and that politics, poverty and ignorance are results and not causes; that a great pain, a huge struggle, is wracking the world today and that all nations must come together, beyond any frontier, and fight fiercely and mercilessly, without any hope of immediate reward. Today one nation cannot be saved alone. If Russia is not saved, Greece cannot be saved. If Bulgaria or Turkey suffers, Greece cannot be saved. We are all one.

But we have to speak to the people with clarity and courage, without evasions and politics. The best policy in these times of dishonesty is honesty.

The idea that we are entering a terrible lengthy Middle Ages, full of cruelty and struggles, keeps ripening in me. What does Middle Ages mean? That one class, the one which rules, wanes and must fall, but it remains solidly organized, it resists, it does not want to give up.

The other class, which does the work and which is unjustly treated, begins to be enlightened, begins to get organized and strives to take over power. But it is still weak because it is incompletely organized and is still hypnotized with the words, ideas and moral values that the ruling class has invented in order to keep it submissive. This in-between period, the period of contention and the rupturing of the equilibrium, is the Middle Ages were are now entering.

Neither we nor our children will see peace. Wars will break out, still nationalistic to begin with, then of a mixed character and finally exclusively between the classes. We must establish deeply in our minds this historical moment we are going through. We have to regulate our energies accordingly. Any attempt at improvement just delays the final victory. It is yet another invention, another ruse of the disguised bourgeoisie. Today we have only one duty — the Overthrow. We must end the stage of discussion where everything is true or right in accordance with logic. The "Overthrow" must go through this first stage — discussion — and enter the second one — the stage of faith — which does not discuss and is not discussed; it simply inflames hearts, gives birth to actions, destroys civilizations, creates new ones. Discussions have never renewed the face of the earth. These are all symptoms of decline and lack of faith. What has always renewed the earth is Passion, enthusiasm and Faith without intellectual argument.

Do we have faith? If we do, Greece is saved. If we don't have it, all the apostolic (Christ-less) campaigns of humans, who are afraid of their own shadows, will end up being ridiculous.

I'm working on *Letters to My Wife*[1] all the time. The first half covers: What is the best of human history, at what historical point we are today, what is the duty of our race and what our individual duty is within the modern struggle. The second part is an application of all this to the School. How our only duty is to prepare children for the future social struggle. All education has a unity, a specific aim, it serves the contemporary needs.

I am writing it with emotion and faith. The idea that I am writing it for you gives me courage and heats my words. I sent you a small "letter"; if you want, you can publish it. I can send you more if you want me to. But I would like you to publish them in the magazine *Noumas*.[2]

I have kept all your letters, arranged according to date. So when you want them you can use them.

How badly I must have formulated my ideas about contemporary mass meetings for you to have misunderstood me to that extent. My God, when I think how imperfect the means of communicating with people are, I am horrified. But what I meant was that every faith (and that is what the communist idea is today, having finished its first stage, the stage of "theory"), every mass enthusiasm must always find new mass ways to externalize its protest, to move, to get aligned. But communism hasn't found this new means yet, that's why it borrows the old archetypes of past gatherings. You should have been there to see how the leaders, instead of riling up the crowd, were quieting it down. The crowd didn't know which way to go, what form to take, or what was going to happen so it scattered. A new type of gathering is needed, wild, organic, with a beginning, middle and an end, a truly vital method. This type of large gathering of the faithful is not yet herè but it will come. This was what I meant and that was what I wrote you about. No one is more disgusted than me with the old, dead masks of divinity — of old religions. The new face of my God, as I have often described it to you, is that of a Worker, who is hungry, who works and revolts. A worker who smells of tobacco and wine, dark and powerful, full of desire and a thirst for revenge. He resembles the old Warlords of the East wearing sheepskins around their legs and with a double axe hanging from their leather belts, a Ghenghis Khan who leads new hungry races and smashes apart the palaces and the cellars of the well-fed and rapes the harems of the impotent. My God is cruel, full of passions and will, without compromises, inflexible. The Earth is his field, sky and earth are one.

I don't waste my time with metaphysics and theories. My metaphysics are a tool, a plough for this earth, a weapon for the modern struggle. My God, how can I express what is in me, so that you can feel what I mean and never misunderstand me again. It's my fault. When I talk about these subjects which eat at my vitals, my thought leaps, I consider as known many unknown things, I burn, I don't have the patience to speak clearly.

But in my second book, *Letters to My Wife*, I'll speak to you exclusively about Religion, Ethics and Art as I imagine them according to our Faith. In my third book I'll speak to you about society (from Russia if I go).

I'm tired, very tired, cherie, I again have symptoms of overwork — heavy stomach, nausea, dizziness. I'll go to some village to rest. In a while the new book, *Letters to My Wife*, will be ready. *Buddha* is coming along and I like it tremendously: It has become something modern, barbarians intervene, Buddha's scope widens.

* * *

Always, always yours, cherie

N.

⊷⊶

LETTER 75

Cherie, your letter caused me great grief and great joy. Grief because I saw how sad and disgusted you are with me. Human beings are wretched, heartless, petty and worthless. But in them I distinguish an essence higher than they are that nevertheless runs them and pushes them on and makes them live and then kills and surpasses them and goes on. What miracles leap up from within this clay! Awe and respect overcome me when I come face to face with the filthy mass which gave birth to divine songs and statues, thoughts, intense loves and sacrifices. It is an unrestrained assault, greater than soldiers, greater than generals, mysterious, without beginning, without end, without aim. Such a mass of clay is humanity, such a mass of clay is each of us. What is our duty? To fight so that a small flower will bloom out of this manure of our flesh and mind, to create a groan, to rise up and want, if only for a moment, to escape from our wretchedness. Do not look at the people around you in the narrow perspective of space and time. Lift them up and place them in a broader circle which they themselves do not see. Look at how, without knowing it (and moreover, without wanting it), they create a work greater than themselves. Can't you see this Work? Fight, blot out details, overcome personal nervousness and triviality; widen as much as you can, the illuminated circle where man struggles on, cursing, acting badly, but forever ascending. The details are always horrible but the sum total is always excruciatingly holy.

I am also disgusted. I don't want to be with people; I speak to them with difficulty and I can't accept their sluggish, craven rhythm. But I love and respect Man, I respect his dark, bloody attempt; I am fighting to give my mind, my life to it, to advance it a little quicker, to make its soul become a little braver.

You say you are anxious about whether you'll find me good and if you'll be able to live with me for a while. I don't know if I'm good or bad. I only know that I suffer more than you know, that nothing personal interests me, that I am giving my whole life in seeking, beyond my personal life, one thing and one thing only. I firmly believe in the nobility and force of a Spirit that passes through plants, animals and 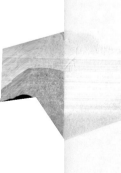en, and that is now battling consciously with me and wants to go beyond me, to be free of my worthless nature, to be rid of me. I struggle to serve this Spirit because I know that *it*, and not this sack of bones, meat, hair and passions that I carry about, is the essence of my soul.

When I tell you that I love you and that I'm waiting for you with indescribable expectation, I feel this Spirit, this God

I believe in, stirring you up and ruling you; because of that I love you and am always with you. We are one, we are one flame in this furnace which burns and transubstantiates Earth. You curse, shout and deny, because you cannot accept God's decline. But you support me and I support you and the two of us support this God who is not onmipotent, so that he will not fall. I no longer have a romantic, theological abstract conception of God. My God is not all-wise, all-good, almighty. He struggles to save himself from his nastiness, from petty passions, easy joys and cowardly hopes. And I feel this struggle of his inside me, I am a small battlefield of his, I live all of his struggle. As I struggle, he struggles, as I ascend, he ascends. Difficult, dreadful, endless is this ascension. I will die in mid-journey but my breath will be united with his breath and it will leap out of the body and continue the march.

"I am your Lord, your God", his Cry rings out in me, "I am not a refuge. I am not a home and a hope. I do not cure illness. I have no pity. I am not good. I am neither Father nor Son. I am your General."

"You are not my slave nor a toy in my hands. You are not my friend nor my child. You are my companion in battle."

"Hold on to the mountain pass with which I entrusted you; do not betray it. You have a duty and can become a hero in your trench."

"Always be uneasy and unadapted. When a habit becomes comfortable, crush it. The greatest sin is pleasure. Where are we going? Will we ever win? Towards what end is all this struggle? Don't ask, Fight!"

Ah! cherie, if only I could overcome your distress by showing you this enormous circle of endless agony. Life is a heroic march, it is no idyll. It is an idyll only for small insignificant souls. Without grumbling, we must pay dearly every moment for the hard privilege of not accepting wretchedness and not capitulating.

Cherie, everything here is waiting for you. Great preparations have taken place. Because you might not like my house I have now rented an excellent room in Kastanakis' house. It is brightly lit and only five minutes from here. Thus you will often be with Mrs. Kastanakis whom you will like a lot. The four of us will eat together, we'll go to Russian cabarets and you'll see dances and Russian women. A month after you come the Kastanakis family will go to Paris for a month and then return here. If you want, we can go with them so you can see Paris. I'll do all I can to be less boring. We'll talk together beautifully, I'll read you a little of *Buddha* and you'll have manuscripts to read me. Only come quickly.

Bring whatever warm clothes you have because you'll be cold. I've ordered a lot of coal for the stove.

Bring all the yellow shirts I have (not white) as well as the manuscript of *Nikiforos Fokas*.[1] Also the *Baedeker India*.

Also the coupons so I can send them to London. Or rather, two or three coupons from every share. Don't come alone because you'll run into difficulties. Arrange something with Skokas or Saridakis or Danilidis who will probably come. Write me quickly without fail. Get your passport in order. My joy at your coming is indescribable.

N.

LETTER 76

Cherie, I read your letter with great joy. But when I put questions to you and when you write me, have my letter in front of you so you are sure to answer them.

1) How was the trip? Any troubles? Did you enjoy Stavrou's company?

2) Did you see snow? I was so unhappy that just the day after you left everything was covered with snow.

3) What are your final impressions of Europe? What will you tell acquaintances?

My own news is still up in the air. I'm thinking of not sending this letter to you until I have something definite to say. Where will I go? Here life becomes more intolerable every day. Zorbas[1] didn't answer. It seems, as you said, that he has become a drifter and the dream of the Serbian mountain has fallen apart. I haven't given up on India yet. I still have to wait five or six days. If this doesn't work either, I'll seek refuge in Southern Italy. I need to come into contact with the Italian intellectual movement and see the outcome of human efforts there.

The organization here is after me to undertake direction of the magazine, with complete freedom. Kastanakis and Danilidis have gone to Paris now to hold a conference and to find money. I've turned it down; I'd accept only if they would allow me to bring out a purely communistic magazine, a thing they don't dare.

I wrote to Dieterich in Leipzig that, if he wants me to, I'll go there for a few days to translate *The Saviors of God* into German. Simos, who had begun it, didn't have the time. I'm in agony waiting for Dieterich's answer. This question is significant for me because this text will be used for the organizing of men who believe as I do and who face their duty towards contemporary necessity the same way I do.

Tonight after I'd been working all day in your little room I leaned tiredly on the stove. I don't know why but a deep bitterness came over me. I thought to myself, "Why all this agony of mine, this grave life, taking ever more intensely this form, the ascetic form of my soul?" It is as though I am the instrument of one higher than me, I do things I don't want to do. I follow orders which are above me, I'm a toy in the hands of the Unknown One who is inside me and who is me, my essence, beyond my ephemeral, worldly essence. This Unknown One I call God. I see him struggling in animals, in men, in the masses you saw becoming frantic in Stadiou Street, who don't clearly know what they want and why they hate or love. I suffer because of this Dark Unknown One; I struggle, I'll fight on as long as I breathe, as long as my flesh is warm, to illuminate him a little, to advance him a little further, to save him from the clay of my body and mind. What? For what? I don't know. I can neither find reasonable arguments nor do I value them. My heart urges me on, a voice inside me, outside me, beyond reason, commands me and I follow with enthusiasm and curses. Upward! Upward! Upward! the Cry shouts. Do not hesitate, do not despair, do not stop. Put your desires in order of priority, keep saying: The most difficult way — that is my way.

Sometimes I can't hold back the tears. But I feel they also are an instrument of the Unseen, because as soon as I cry a few "gentle tears", the calm ones without sobbing, I feel lighter straight off and again I start on my uphill way. My only deep human consolation now is that you came to see me. This continually takes root in me, is made secure, gives me warmth and joy. A human being who loves me came and gave me warm pyjamas which I'm now wearing, she knitted me a woolen vest so I wouldn't get cold and she spoke to me, caring that I exist. Ah! my God, how all this concern consoles me, I know I'm not worthy of her, but human love overlooks things and fills even the most worthless man with regal happiness. The good which you did me was, I would think, the greatest happiness of my life. May God keep you well, grant you the strength (without upset, without faint-heartedness) to be brave in the struggle on this earth!

* * *

Always yours

N.

LETTER 83
(sent from Assisi, Italy)

Cherie, again great joy from your letter. I also got the Baedeker, the magazines and the newspapers. Your letter in *Foni tou Efedrou*[1] was very powerful, all passion and feeling. Tomorrow, I'll sit down and write them a letter myself to give them courage. They must be simple men and the "intellectuals" of Heraklion will laugh at them. It is, therefore, a good and courageous act for the two of us to stand on their side. If I can, I'll write them when I come down to Crete. I like to give our opinion thus and illuminate things as much as we can in our small homeland. "To hate, to be implacable" these two motifs of your letter correspond perfectly to my soul. I'll write them about the necessity of this whole struggle and the need to transubstantiate it into an unshakeable faith that we will win. We'll win, not because it is "right" and "moral" that people shouldn't suffer, not only for that, but because, above all, wanting it or not, realizing it or not, this is the invincible rhythm of human history.

I'll try to write them a short and simple letter.

* * *

My life goes on here as always. All day writing and working and when there is sun I go for a walk in the olive groves or to the various monasteries. I have come to know several Capuchins and we talk about theology, St. Francis and miracles. And sometimes we go to the presbytery of a friend of the Capuchins and go down to the basement and drink a glass of wine, the three Capuchins and me.

They take me to be very wise and I use the famous anecdote of Lekatsas and say that I am the least among Greek intellectuals.

Did you read Joergensen's *St. Francis* that we have at the house? The saint was not as effeminate and tender as the biographers and scholarly exploiters want to present him to us. He was completely insistent, stubborn and convinced and he became very fierce when his purpose was opposed. He was a great, an ideal communist. He saw that the source of all evil was in private property and he forbade (this is the basis of his order) his pupils to have any kind of private property, large or small. They lived by their work and when they didn't have any, they begged. During that time — around 1200 — there were great social struggles here between the fat (rich) and the lean, between big and small (*majores* and *minores*). St. Francis heroically took the side of the poor; he called his order *minores* and forced the rich in Assisi to bow down to him.

When he first started to preach here in the market (it is preserved unchanged as it was and so is the house of Francis) they attacked him with stones and jeers. After three years he had a pupil — Bernardo, and slowly added two or three others. They had nothing. They slept in a ruin (which is now a splendid church), the water came in through the roof, it was cold, they had no cover and there was snow. This so-called pastoral saint was a miracle of insistence, endurance and intolerance. Slowly he imposed himself. He sent his students to preach all over Italy and later to France, Spain, Morocco, Egypt and Palestine. They built monasteries and huge orders took shape with these three principles: Total poverty, obedience and chastity.

Blind, on the point of death in one corner of a garden on a plank, sleepless from pain and the abundant mice which ran over him, St. Francis one night composed the famous paean of joy, his most brilliant poem: *Laudato tii mi Signore per il fratello il sole* . . . (Be blessed my Lord for brother sun . . .)

Today, ideals and means have changed. But one thing eternal is left, the big mystery of life which is not only pan-human in all times and places but even way before man: Nothing can happen without faith. Faith in its broadest meaning, that is, a firm endurance in the struggle. To argue about communism, to argue pedantically about words, is worthless to the struggle. To believe, to create a soul that is simpler and deeper, different from that of the bourgeoisie, and not to argue with it but to use the so-called dialectic as an ally. To flame — not to argue — to look, to live, to work completely differently from the bourgeoisie — these are all the sure signs of victory.

This conviction grows ever stronger in me. The more secure and enriched my mind becomes, the more intensely I feel that only faith can renew the face of the earth.

Again, I have been carried away by things which you know better than I do. But this is a sign of my spiritual development. Sometimes the blood rushes to my head, I am dominated by the conviction that there is only one remaining duty for me: To follow, like St. Francis, the road which renews life. The other night, in my bed, for the very first time in my life, I had a very short but very intense fainting fit. But in the morning I was completely well and only the terrible sensation of losing my senses remained. Maybe if I wasn't so healthy I would follow this difficult road with more ease. We'll see. Write to me about Zorbas, what is happening? Why does he not write?

* * *

N.

Notes

Introduction

1. Galatea Kazantzakis (nee Alexiou), born in Heraklion, Crete, in 1886, married Nikos Kazantzakis in 1911. They were divorced in 1924. (Galatea later married the poet and critic Markos Avgeris.) She wrote numerous short stories, plays and novels in a lively style, mostly describing the lower and less fortunate classes of society, especially the women. Her collected plays, seventeen in all, were published in 1957. Her best-known novel, *Men and Supermen* (1957), is semi-autobiographical since the hero is obviously meant to be Nikos Kazantzakis, portrayed in a rather critical fashion. She died in 1962.

2. Nikos Kazantzakis, *Symposio*, (Athens, 1977, Editions Eleni Kazantzakis).

3. Nikos Kazantzakis published his first work, a lyrical prose novella entitled *The Snake and the Lily*, in Athens in 1906, under the pseudonym Karmas Nirvanas. In the same year Galatea Kazantzakis, under the pseudonym Lalo de Castro, published an essay entitled "The Sickness of the Century" in the magazine *Pinakothiki*.

4. Kazantzakis had two sisters, Anastasia (born 1884) and Eleni (born 1887).

5. In 1914 he went to Mount Athos, accompanied by his friend the poet Angelos Sikelianos. Between 1915 and 1917 he travelled extensively around Greece and in 1917 he went to Switzerland. During 1919-1920 he was in the Caucasus, supervising the repatriation of Greek refugees. In 1920 he visited Paris and spent most of 1921-1924 in Austria, Germany and Italy.

6. Nikos Kazantzakis, *Spain*, trans. Amy Mims (New York, Simon and Schuster, 1963), p. 11.

7. Nikos Kazantzakis, *Epistoles pros ten Galateia*, (Athens, Diphros, 1958), letter 26, p. 61.

8. Ibid, letter 13, p. 21.

9. Ibid, letter 41, p. 104.

10. Ibid, letter 41, p. 107.

11. Ibid, letter 41, p. 107.

12. Ibid, letter 32, p. 77.

13. Ibid, letter 26, p. 63.

14. Ibid, letter 48, p. 133.

15. Helen Kazantzakis, *Nikos Kazantzakis: A Biography*, trans. Amy Mims (New York, Simon and Schuster, 1968), p. 171.

16. Nikos Kazantzakis, *The Saviors of God: Spiritual Exercises*, trans. and intro. Kimon Friar (New York, Simon and Schuster, 1960), p. 101.

17. Ibid, p. 54.

18. Ibid.

19. Ibid, p. 118.

Letters to Papastephanou

LETTER 5

1. A book that was never written.

LETTER 7

1. A tragedy written around 1915, first published in 1928.

Letters to Galatea

LETTER 13

1. "The troupe" was how Kazantzakis referred to Galatea's women friends.

LETTER 15

1. Kazantzakis customarily addressed his wife in letters with the French word.

2. Dora Ladas, daughter of Professor Georgios Ladas (1852-1914) was one of Galatea's friends.

LETTER 17

1. It was never published nor is it probable that he ever finished it.

2. "Shortcomings" that Galatea, being so different from Kazantzakis, attributed to him.

3. By this he means, Austria becoming communist.

4. Demosthenes Danilidis was a lifelong friend of Kazantzakis.

LETTER 19

1. Ioannis Anghelakis, a lawyer and close friend of Kazantzakis, who was also a member of the mission to the Caucasus.

2. Navsika, daughter of the poet Kostis Palamas.

3. Anghelos Sikelianos (1884-1951), a eminent Greek poet. Kazantzakis met him in 1914 and they became very close friends and remained so despite later ideological disagreements.

4. Georgios Vendiris (1890-1957), Greek writer best known for his *Biography of Eleftherios Venizelos*.

LETTER 29

1. Dimitris Dimitrakos, Athens publisher, who had engaged Kazantzakis to compile various material for books, such as children's stories. He never published anything by Kazantzakis himself except *Alexis Zorbas*.

LETTER 40

1. Nikolaos Plastiras, colonel in the Greek army, headed the revolution which followed the Asia Minor disaster in 1922. On his instigation six prominent politicians and generals were arrested, were found responsible for the disaster and were executed.

LETTER 41

1. Kazantzakis started writing his tragedy *Buddha* in Vienna in 1922. Under the influence of communist ideology he destroyed the original and rewrote it in a more savage and bitter form. He completed it in 1941 but it was not published until 1956 in the series of his complete works (Athens, Diphros).

2. Lefteris Alexiou, born 1890, poet, brother of Galatea.

3. Markos Avgeris, left wing poet and critic. He first met Kazantzakis in 1905 and Galatea in 1910. He became Galatea's second husband in 1933.

4. Kostas Varnalis, born 1884, was a well-known communist poet.

5. Kostas Sfakianakis (1890-1946), Cretan-born composer and musicologist, specializing in Byzantine music.

LETTER 44

1. Dore, a fashionable cafe at that time.

2. Schestov, the famous utopian philosopher.

LETTER 47

1. After the defeat of the Greek army by the Turks in 1922 and the destruction of Smyrna thousands of Greeks were forced to flee to the neighboring islands or mainland Greece. It was the end of 2,500 years of Greek settlement on the Aegean coasts of Asia Minor and the end of the Great Idea, that is, the dream of the Greeks of regaining the territories which had once formed the Byzantine Empire.

LETTER 48

1. *Asketiki*, subtitled *The Saviors of God*, a lyrical-philosophical work which summarizes his ideas on man and the world, begun in Vienna and completed in Berlin in 1923. It was first published in *Renaissance* magazine, Athens, 1927. It was first published in English in 1960. See note 16 to the Introduction, above.

LETTER 51

1. Sotiris Skipis, Greek satirical poet.

LETTER 54

1. Photios Kondoglou (Kontoglou) was an important modern Greek artist and iconographer as well as author; his work drew from late Byzantine prototypes and Greek folklore and is characterized by a preoccupation with spiritual themes.

LETTER 60

1. From Dhemel's poem, *Der Arbeitsmann*.

2. Sent Mahesa, a celebrated Indian religious dancer.

LETTER 63

1. Mrs. Myrsini Kleanthous was an acquaintance of Kazantzakis. Georgios Papandreou, politician and later Prime Minister, played a leading role in Greek politics for half a century. The plural is used to indicate contempt.

2. "We have to go back, retreat. The concessions we have made are not enough. Let us recognize our errors. We have reached a point of regression not only with regard to capitalism but also to the organization of commerce and the

acceptance of money. So we must look danger in the face and not hide our retreat from the working class."

3. I.e. the Hellespont. In August 1919 Kazantzakis was appointed Director General of the Ministry of Social Assistance by Venizelos and head of the mission for the repatriation of Greeks from the Caucasus, where they had been persecuted by the Bolsheviks. Kazantzakis and his team successfully brought some 150,000 refugees back to Greece.

LETTER 66

1. A work that was never completed.

2. It was the leading literary magazine of the 1920's and was strongly influenced by Kostis Palamas.

LETTER 75

1. *Nikiphoros Fokas*, a tragedy written in 1916, first published in 1927.

LETTER 76

1. Georgios Zorbas, the inspiration for one of Kazantzakis' most famous novels, *Alexis Zorbas*, published in English as *Zorba the Greek* (New York, Simon and Schuster, 1953). Zorbas was a Greek worker whom Kazantzakis met in 1917 and with whom he undertook the exploitation of a lignite mine in the Mani, in the Peloponnesus. The enterprise was a failure but the experience provided the material for one of Kazantzakis' most widely read novels.

LETTER 83

1. A newspaper published in Heraklion by a group of veterans of the Asia Minor disaster.

LNT   R/EIOZPF
                              KAZANTZAKIS